God's Healing River

by
Jack Sheffield

God's Healing River

Inquiries should be addressed to

www.deepriverministries.com

First Printing September 2003
Second Printing June 2004
Third Printing September 2006
Fourth Printing March 2008
Fifth Printing April 2009

Cataloging-in-Publication Data

Sheffield, Jack
God's Healing River

    p.   cm.

ISBN 978-09727208-1-6

1. Religious aspects--Christianity   2. God   3. Faith
4. Faith and reason--21st Century   5. Forgiveness

I. Title II. Author III. Monograph

BT 100 B65   291.4sh

Library of Congress Catalog Card Number: 2003096468

Printed in the United States of America
at Morgan Printing in Austin, Texas

Acknowledgements

I want to express my sincere, heartfelt thanks to...

My beloved wife Anna Marie who is the love of my youth and my stay.

My mom, Mary Sheffield. Thank you for a lifetime believing in and living out the beautiful things in life.

Our dear friends Linda and Don Wukasch, Jim and Sharon Austin, Bill and Linda Dreyer, Ginger Baker, Mary Ann Kelly, Kay Barbour, Bitsy Rubsamen, Dr. Carl and Pat Peveto, Jack and Marilyn Curran, Karen Belinne, and so many others who believed with us and have been the best friends a person could have.

Norma Dearing who is a bright light shining in the night. She inspires so many with her wit, charm, and humor; for her love of God.

My Lord Jesus, who said to me, "Go... and I am with you always..."

Matt. 28:19-20

Foreword

Many years ago God invited Jack Sheffield to come into His river of healing. Fortunately for himself and the many thousand recipients of his ministry, Jack answered that call. And he wasn't satisfied like many of us to stick in his toe or even to wade, but he moved deeper and deeper into the water until he became immersed in God's Spirit and truth.

This book is a virtual reservoir of knowledge, of experience with and practical insight into hearing God and moving in His power. God has called Jack to great things, but it has not always been without cost. The testimony of his personal car accident and death encounter reveals his understanding of the supernatural in a way no one can refute or forget.

His wealth of experience, stories and testimonies will make you laugh, cry, want to jump for joy and get yourself to the river. There are sections of the book that are practical and helpful for every Christian, like the power of forgiveness and examples of God's holiness and entering into His presence. The description and explanation of what actually takes place when the Holy Spirit comes in power for healing is beautifully developed.

Hearing God in prophecy and dreams and understanding the correlation between prophecy and prayer only help us go deeper into understanding God's Holy Spirit gifts for healing. God's Healing River shares the heart of God and His longing to loose His Holy Spirit over each one of us.

God has placed His vision in Jack's heart that churches are to be places of healing, restoration and redemption and that He desires using ordinary lay people to bring it forth—people like you and me. Jack shows us in this wonderful book that when we believe and pray, God shows up in power. We become transformed, never again content to sit on the banks idly observing this living water flowing by us. We desire to go deeper, to become immersed in His love, power, grace and healing. By doing this we become a tributary of this river, a body of living water to be used by our Father God.

Norma Dearing
Radio Broadcaster and
Author of The Healing Touch

Table of Contents

Introduction

Then he brought me back to the en-
trance of the temple; there, water was
flowing from below the threshold of
the temple toward the east (for the
temple faced east); and the water was
flowing down from below the south
end of the threshold of the temple,
south of the altar going on eastward
with a cord in his hand, the man measured one thousand cubits, and then
led me through the water; and it was
ankle-deep. Again he measured one
thousand, and led me through the
water; and it was up to the waist.
Again he measured one thousand, and
it was a river that I could not cross,
for the water had risen; it was deep
enough to swim in, a river that could
not be crossed. He said to me, 'Mortal, have you seen this?' Then he led

me back along the bank of the river. As I came back, I saw on the bank of the river a great many trees on the one side and on the other. He said to me, 'This water flows toward the eastern regions and goes down in to the Arabah, and when it enters the sea, the sea of stagnant waters, and the water will become fresh. Wherever the river goes, every living creature that swarms will live, and there will be very many fish, once these waters reach there. It will become fresh; and everything will live where the river goes.

Ezekiel 47:1-2, 3-9

This is one of the most powerful visions in the whole Bible. It was written in Babylon somewhere between 622-600 B.C. It has to do with the restoration of all things in God's fallen creation. In this forty-seventh chapter of his prophesies the prophet Ezekiel sees a body of water that is God's Healing River. The river flows out to the east from the altar in the temple of God. It becomes a DEEP river where its banks are lined with trees that sweeten the bitter waters of life, and everywhere this river goes, it brings healing so that all living creatures flourish in its waters.

This river is a perfect representation of the present day healing ministry of Jesus Christ of Nazareth. His ministry is going forth even today from God's throne into all nations; he is bringing restoration to all things. There have been many references to this river in our generation, particularly with respect to the notion of revival, or spiritual awakening for our times. On closer observation of the text it becomes apparent that Ezekiel is talking about the subject of healing. A person, whom I think is Jesus Himself, is standing out in the middle of the river and is calling to Ezekiel to come on out into the waters. This river starts out shallow and gradually becomes so deep and wide that a person could swim in it. The river is a very important metaphor for a coming spiritual surge of the manifest glory and power of God that will rival all previous moves of God in former generations. It is my belief that God is calling His people in this country out into a river of healing that will overflow its banks and begin to restore the nations of the earth in a mighty flood of mercy and grace. The river has already broken its banks in other parts of the world, but there is still a greater glory of salvation to come. Ezekiel is saying that the true nature of salvation involves the healing of individuals, families, communities, cities, and ultimately the nations of the world. Therefore, we have chosen the title *God's Healing River.*

The Gospel of John is a major inspiration for this work. Some date John's account of the life of Jesus to as late as 100 A.D. It is strikingly different from the other three Gospels of Matthew, Mark, and Luke that were written much earlier. The purpose of the Gospel of John is very clear,

> **Now Jesus did many other signs in the presence of the disciples, which are not written in this book; but these are written that you may believe that Jesus is the Christ, the Son of God, and that believing you may have life in His name.**
>
> **(John 20:30-31)**

That life, or *Zoe* in the Greek language, is eternal and begins now for the believer. It is not just the future event of going to heaven. *Zoe* embodies the vast richness of a present day salvation to include deliverance from evil and darkness, protection from harm, healing from diseases and distresses, preservation of all that is good and holy, and provision of any substance needed to further the purpose of God in abundant living. Salvation this full and wondrous belongs to everyone who calls upon the name of the Lord Jesus.

The format of this work follows the Gospel of John. In essence, John wrote a narrative of eight signs performed by Jesus of Nazareth satisfying the question of who this man is. They are:

1. Turning Water into Wine.
2. The Nobleman's Son.
3. Raising the paralyzed man at the Pool of Bethesda.
4. Feeding the five thousand.
5. Walking on the Water.
6. Healing the blind man blind from birth.
7. Raising Lazareth from the dead.
8. Jesus is raised from the dead and appears to many.

Biblical teachers today believe that John laid out these signs as a skeleton to build his good news on. He used each one as an opportunity to flesh out truth and teach all around these miracles. Each miracle is seen as a powerful allegorical illustration of the way life comes forth in the believer. We should like to do the same thing with eight signs in our times, our lives and ministries where Jesus has reminded us of and demonstrated His power and mercy for the purpose of opening our eyes, and turning us to Him that he might heal us. It is the intent of this work to testify to the saving and healing power of God available to every person who asks, to further the work of the Kingdom of God in preaching the good news, healing the sick, and delivering all those oppressed of the evil one. These manifest "giftings," or miracles provide a rich base for teaching the practical and do-able aspects of Christian Healing.

The message of the Gospel of healing has spread around the world at a quantum pace. The healing ministry has grown over the past thirty years since Agnes Sanford was writing her books and Francis MacNutt was beginning to introduce healing as a realistic part of church experience and practice. The Body of Christ is no longer just interested in or intrigued by the supernatural power of God to heal, and in how the "professionals" do it. In recognizing the priesthood of all believers, all lay ministers are begging for active participation in the work of the church. Many are awakening to their own calling and gifts, and are poised to join the procession being readied for the greatest harvest the world has ever known. This harvest will be attended with marvelous signs and wonders, healings, deliverances, and special "anointings" of supernatural provision from heaven. Besides wanting to inspire the reader with real-life situations and settings where God has proven Himself faithful and strong, one of the goals of this book is to bring its readers into a deeper appreciation for their part in the modern day narrative of God's intervention into the lives of hurting and desperate people.

We are at the brink of an enormous spiritual breakthrough in this time, even in a prophetic time-line, where we are, with a clarion call, being invited to swim in This River of God, over our heads, swept up in the currents of His fathomless love. **"There is a River whose streams make glad the city of God." Psalm 46:4** Many want to know how to participate in the move of God in our time. This book answers some of the questions people have about the Holy Spirit and how God is moving today to heal the nations. You will learn:

- How faith comes to the believer.
- How healing comes.
- The greatest help to prayer: prophecy.
- The test for truly "hearing" God.
- How to discern the true Presence of God.

8 God's Healing River

- Why sometimes obedience precedes faith.
- How to break past spiritual barriers and "stuckness."
- What it means to swim in God's Healing River.
- How to enter the most glorious enterprise in all the earth: the Harvest.
- What the "fourth voice" is in worship.

CHAPTER ONE

Signs, Signs, Everywhere are Signs

First Sign

There were many signs and wonders in the early church. **"And God did extraordinary miracles by the hands of Paul, so that handkerchiefs or aprons were carried away from his body to the sick, and diseases left them and the evil spirits came out of them."** Acts 19:11-12 Of the apostles, especially Peter, it was said,

> Now many signs and wonders were done among the people by the hands of the apostles. And they were all together in Solomon's Portico. None of the rest dared join them, but the people held them in high honor. And more than ever believers were added

to the Lord, multitudes both of men and women, so that they even carried out the sick in to the streets, and laid them onto beds and pallets, that as Peter came by at least his shadow might fall on some of them. The people also gathered from the towns around Jerusalem, bringing the sick and those afflicted with unclean spirits, and they were all healed.

Acts 5: 12-16

These signs were irrefutable evidence of the mighty hand of the Lord being with his people.

In 1981 the most incredible "over-our-heads" event took place early in our ministry. It was a baptism in God's Healing River and a sign of what is to come. It was an expression of the marvelous nature of the surprises of the Holy Spirit. These surprises often come to those whose only qualification is having a heart for what God wants. The healing ministry is not only about reading books and attending seminars. It is so much better than that! Right away, early in our ministry, God gave to Anna Marie and me an experience that far surpassed anything we had ever heard about. We caught a brief glimpse of what I believe will be an ongoing experience for multitudes in the days that are right before us. **There is coming a gathering of the greatest harvest the world or the kingdom of God has ever seen, and it will be accompanied by mighty signs and wonders, healings and miracles bathed in the GLORY OF GOD.**

Novices

In terms of maturity and authority in ministry, we were only in up to our ankles in God. We were in God's wading pool. We were naïve in many ways, knowing very little about God's word and power. I was just a babe in Christ, new in the ministry as a deacon in the Methodist Church. I was still in seminary at Perkins School of Theology in Dallas at SMU when this event took place. We were just beginning to see the healing power of God work in our midst, but God would not wait for us to become spiritual giants for what was about to happen. God intended to demonstrate for us what an immersion in blessing looked like, a saturation of His direct presence. The Lord God was ready to pour out an unfathomable experience of HIS GLORY and MIGHT. Because we were so inept in ministry skills, innocent, and absolutely unprepared, it may serve to encourage some who are tentative and fearful about entering into the most important ministry in the earth: reconciling people to God and seeing God heal them spirit, soul, and body.

"In Over Our Heads"

Inez was a parishioner with whom I had been working in the area of healing. She had terrible food allergies. For example, if she ate any corn products she would land in the hospital with a severe allergic reaction. At communion one day, God zapped her with about five thousand volts of His power and she shook all the way home. She made two pans of cornbread and ate one whole pan. She was so healed that she never had allergies of that kind again.

One Sunday night Inez and a few of us were down at the church for a talk on healing. She stood up in the middle of my talk and asked for prayer. She felt a tremendous burden for her nephew who had been shot in a hunting accident, so we brought her to the front of the church and prayerfully laid hands on her in proxy for her nephew.

And then it HAPPENED. All of a sudden, my hands began to burn like fire. I don't mean a little warm sensation came into my hands, or some tingling feeling. They felt like they were on fire. I looked up to try to find my dear friend John Mark

Searcy. The GLORY of God was right there. I could barely see his face for the soft golden light that so brilliantly filled the area of the sanctuary where we were ministering to Inez. I said, "John Mark, do you see what I see?" He said, "Yes, yes, I do," and I said the strangest thing I think I've ever said: "People, God is in this room, ask Him what you will, but be careful what you ask."

The Shekinah

And he raised up the court all around the tabernacle and the altar, and hung up the screen of the court gate. So Moses finished the work. Then the cloud [The Shekinah] covered the tabernacle of meeting, and the glory of the Lord filled the tabernacle. And Moses was not able to enter the tabernacle of meeting, because the cloud rested above it, and the glory of the Lord filled the tabernacle.

Exodus 40:33-35

Amazingly, God's *Shekinah* glory, the same golden effusive light that shown over the mercy seat in the tabernacle on top of the Ark of the Covenant, was engulfing the entire front of this little Methodist church. Moses had written about this very thing thousands of years ago.

The Glory of the Lord, the same *Shekinah* Moses saw, is a very real and tangible "substance." Dictionaries define glory as exaltation, high honor, or something worthy of praise. Closer to a definition is majestic radiance, splendor, or brightness. But these are inadequate in describing what we saw. It was a real "substance" that filled the air. The scripture talks about the "weight" of His glory as though it is a material object. It was sublime, and it was a wonder-filled luminous display attesting to the magnificence of our Lord Jesus. This is the "substance" that the apostle Peter would write about it in one of his epistles,

> **For we did not follow cleverly devised myths, when we made known to you the power and coming of our lord Jesus Christ, but we were eyewitnesses of his majesty. For when he received honor and glory from God the Father and the voice was borne to him by the Majestic Glory, 'This is my beloved Son, with whom I am well pleased,' we heard this voice borne from heaven, for we were with him on the holy mountain. And we have the**

prophetic word made more sure. You do well to pay attention to this as a lamp shining in a dark place, until the day dawns and the morning star rises in your hearts.

2 Peter 1:16-19

This event for the display of God's glory on Jesus was real, memorable, and irrefutable in the minds of the apostles, and we found ourselves breathing the same rarified air, and consumed with the exact same majesty. We did well to pay heed.

Inez came to the healing service that night out of concern for a loved one; she would have her wildest dreams come true. **"Ask Him what you will. . ."** In stunned silence, we held hands, and waited a few seconds. Mary, our pianist, then began to share that her husband had come to church that night with kidney stones. He was in intense pain and on painkillers. As though dazed, yet with a childlike expression, Mary's husband gently asked to be healed. Instantly the man was completely and totally healed. There was no pain left at all. His wife, being amazed, then said, "Lord, my son has been so sick with the flu, and his phone is broken; will you go and touch him and heal him?" She could not call him to check on him before she got to the church because the phones in that area of town were down. She prayed for him, and found out when she got home that during that same time that she prayed for him, he sat up and felt completely well. She also found his phone working when he called her to tell her about how good he felt. God even cared about his phone!

Of course we prayed for Inez' nephew and his plight, and later Inez told us that night he sat up and asked for a hamburger to eat. They removed the tube; he ate, and kept the food down with no problems whatsoever! Glory, LITERALLY, Glory To God!!

Jesus and the People Swam in this River

The impact of this event reminded me of the Scriptures where Jesus would bring such a mighty presence of healing light to communities in Israel that everyone, not just a few, but everyone would be healed. In Matthew it says something so great, "**Jesus... withdrew.... And many followed him, and he healed them all...**" **Matthew 12:15** ALL of them were healed. What a marvelous power it is! This is what John meant when he said, "**... we have beheld His glory, glory as of the only begotten of the Father.**" **(John 1:14)** The glory of God was on him so strong that the sick and dying people were in over-their-heads in the River of God's miraculous power and healing presence. I will never forget that night and what happened to us. It is forever etched in my memory banks as the most remarkable experience of my Christian walk. This was a complete immersion in healing light. We SWAM in God's Healing River for this brief period of time. Everything we asked came to pass. All sick in that room who were prayed for, and even those not present, were healed. All of them!

A Sign of Things to Come

Many times I have asked, "God, why did you show us such an incredible demonstration and display of your glory, and then it was gone?" Was this a happening that is supposed to occur on a regular basis? Is this something we can expect to happen again? We had never seen anything like it, that defined, or that pronounced. Since then, we have been in some fabulous meetings where we were much aware of the fire of God and where the healing presence was very strong, but this was a special sign. I had to ask, was it the prayer time we had been devoting to God so consistently that brought the power and the glory? Why this brief torrential outpouring, and then back to business as usual in the more shallow streams of church life, committee meetings, and "normal" occasions of God's merciful blessings?

It was very close to the Transfiguration experience like Peter, James, and John had on the mountaintop with Jesus when Moses and Elijah showed up and Jesus' garments began to sparkle brighter than the noonday after the manifest Glory came upon him. Only this time it was on his "body" in its present form on the earth. **"For where two or three are gathered in my name, I am there among them." Matthew 18:20** We were a small body, but available. It was a heavenly encounter for sure, and, after that I wanted to live there in that deep water of healing. I was *ruined,* never again content to have church as usual! I wanted the whole church and all the surrounding community to have that same divine presence over us, and to have all their burdens obliterated, their bondages broken, and diseases healed.

I look back on this "close encounter" with God of the first kind, and it reminds me of the prophecy in the Old Testament, **"The later splendor of the house shall be greater than the former." (Haggai 2:9)** It is my firm conviction that we are in that place, that we are beginning to see the later splendor of God's house, and that the first taste for me and for Anna Marie, personally, was that unforgettable moment in a little Methodist student church in 1981.

Recently, in a healing conference, Francis MacNutt said something very important. He said that when we forbid the gifts of the Holy Spirit from operating in the Church, we are robbing the people of God of their heritage and their right to be healed and made whole. I believe it is to deny the true glory of our existence. The highest form of life is to exhibit the greatest potential that resides within. The radiance, splendor, and even magnificence of being human are to be one with the maker, the architect of all existence, and to meet the potential of all that lives within us. Milt Green used to say, "I always figured that anybody who made something could fix it." Well, life in Jesus Christ is more than just being "fixed." It is a life of discovering and unveiling the true glory of our being. Winston Churchill said it this way, "I may be a worm, but I am a glowworm." God wants us to be His personal vessels, manifesting His authority and power to the principalities and rulers of the air that, for now, rule over our cities, towns, and the nations of the world. It is for pulling them down, so the kingdoms of this world become the kingdoms of our God and our savior Jesus Christ. There is no higher form of existence in the world than to meet the full potential of why we were created and to strive towards that end.

God poured out His mighty river at Pentecost upon the first church 2000 years ago after a four hundred year famine for the hearing of the Word of the Lord. The early church met the potential God had planted in them as Jesus washed them and sanctified them in the Word for three and one/half years. They SWAM in God's Healing River right from the beginning! The early disciples were drunk in favor and blessing. The Glory of the Lord rose up on the disciples and ALL of the followers of Jesus. The floodgates opened wide and a torrent of deliverance from evil forces, supernatural provision from heaven, protection by angelic visitation, and prophetic revelation was loosed into the world. **In two years one-third of Jerusalem was won to Christ.** That is a figure of twenty thousand people out of a populace of sixty thousand. It was as though Noah's flood of judgment in Genesis 7:6 became mercy, power, and healing instead of destruction. For several centuries the firmament above rained down a flood of healing and miracles and it burst forth from the firmament beneath with subterranean wells of revelation and knowledge to make a vast expanse of deliverance and freedom washing away sin, disease, sickness and death. It formed a mighty river that swept through the Roman Empire transforming one province after another, one city after another. In less than ninety years one-fifth of the Roman Empire had been captured by the Gospel. According to Tertullian, an early church father, God's Healing River so overran its banks, it reached as far as Great Britain by the year 200 A.D. There were known persecutions in Gaul in 177, and a number of Christians fled northwards to the British Isles.

It took the power of the Holy Spirit to convert the heathen hordes. There was no force as strong in all the earth. Caesar's army was nothing in the face of this massive and overwhelming power of love and forgiveness, of peace and of divine reconciliation. The church was in its infancy; yet it was drenched in giftings, demonstrations, prophecy, operations of the Spirit, and powerful explosions that rocked whole cities like Ephesus, Corinth, and Rome. I sense that more than anything in all the earth, that God wants a repeat performance of GLORY: the divine profusion of healing power that was poured out in that first and second century.

Questions for Small Group Discussion

1. Have you ever seen God's glory? God's glory is the display of His nature, His splendor, radiance, and power. All creation is full of His glory.

3. How are our eyes are dimmed, even blinded to the glory of God's creation?

4. Is the Church the natural house for God's glory to be revealed?

5. How do you respond to this statement: miracles and healings come out of the glory of God?

6. Glory is increasing in the house of God, as the world grows darker in sin and rebellion against God.

7. How does fear restrict the manifestation of God's glory?

CHAPTER TWO

"Simple Faith Moves Mountains"

Second Sign

My wife gets her hair done at Senon's in Austin, Texas. That is the place you want to be, because she comes out looking like a million bucks. This guy is good. As Anna Marie was getting to know Senon, he opened up to share with her that his little six-month-old boy was having somewhere between twenty-five to fifty seizures a day. The little boy was so ill. She asked Senon if they had a church family to walk with them through this terribly difficult time, and he said, "No, we have not been to church in quite some time." (So many are in this place today in our society.) Anna Marie asked if he would come to our church, and let us love on them and pray with them for their little boy. To our great delight, they came within several Sundays of that hair appointment.

When they walked into our traditional service, the room was filled with compassion for this little child. He was so obviously sick, swollen cheeks from steroids, glassy eyes, limp headed. Our hearts were melted, and somehow we all became one in ministering love and prayers to this family. The compassion of Jesus was so thick in the room it was like a cloud or mist of presence.

After the service, we asked the family to come to my office for prayer. Suddenly, the atmosphere changed. There was no tangible anointing, and one could not have felt colder. It greatly puzzled me that what was in the sanctuary had completely lifted off of us. We were left with the stark reality of this child's very serious condition. I thought, when left with no urgings or promptings, and no sure faith directive, just obey the scriptures, and faith will follow. I turned to the Book! I asked if I could read:

Are any among you sick? They should call for the elders of the church and have them pray over them, anointing them with oil in the name of the Lord. The prayer of faith will save the sick, and the Lord will raise them up....

James 5:14-15.a

I asked Senon if I could **obey** those scriptures? He said, "Yes, of course." I took the oil and anointed Sante's little forehead and prayed the prayer of faith: "Thank you Lord for touching this child and healing him in the name of the Lord Jesus Christ of Nazareth." Then it happened, the anointing oil of heaven fell on that room. A flood of tears flowed from everyone there. The fragrance of Jesus filled the air, and we just knew something wonderful had happened.

The next Sunday, Senon and his family came back to church. I could not help but notice that the little one was looking up, and that the people were all cooing over him and excited to see them. I rushed to see them at the end of the service only to find the young parents in a quandary. "How is it going?" I asked. "Oh Father Jack, we are so concerned," they replied, "Sante (whose name means wholeness in Spanish) only had one half of a seizure on Tuesday." I said, "This is bad?" And they informed me of their concern about the medicines he was taking, they were so strong, and they felt God was "messing" with this child. "What do we do?" they asked. Well, I told them to take him to the specialist they had for Sante in San Antonio, and the real miracle was that they got right in to see the doctor.

The specialist examined Sante for several hours. Afterwards he came out with little Sante playing with his nose. The doctor said, "OK, who switched kids on me? Where is the real Sante?" They had run test after test, EEG's, blood work, all of it, and there was no sign of the disease! Glory to God! Sante has not had a seizure since the minor episode on that Tuesday. He is, to this day, the brightest and healthiest "whole" person you have ever seen. What a joy and a delight to see the mighty hand of God move in such a dire situation like the one this precious family faced.

This was an extraordinary sign to our community. Senon's whole family was greatly impacted by this miraculous healing. The family was brought closer than they had ever been. Relationships were mended. I am certain that the effect of his healing will go on for years to come. And this caused me to think of how many people are facing trials they cannot bear or endure. Recently, we prayed for a mother and her son who is twelve years old. The child had diabetes, hardening of the arteries, and heart disease. Can you imagine, twelve years old? People are hurting today, and the more we travel, the more we hear the universal cry for help. Where are people to go? Is there any help when the doctors say the virus has mutated and there are no drugs strong enough to stop the disease from ravaging the loved one's body? Is there no place to go when all hope is gone? The Church must become the healing house of God again, for God's sake.

Fearfully and Wonderfully Made

This healing event caused me to reflect on how fabulous the human being is, even though many people today are living a lifeless, loveless, and joyless existence filled with stress, anxiety, and unhappiness. We seek to fill up our emptiness with more gadgets, bigger salaries, or greater thrills involving sensuality and pleasure. But God did not design us for such a state of being. Our spirit, soul, and body were designed to house health and wholeness. According to the psalmist,

For it was you who formed my inward parts; you knit me together in my mother's womb. I praise you, for I am fearfully and wonderfully made. Wonderful are your works; that I know very well. My frame was not hidden from you, when I was being made in secret,

intricately woven in the depths of the earth.

Psalm 139:14-15

Our neurology and biochemistry function at optimum levels of hormonal and enzymatic activity when we are peaceful, happy, contented, and satisfied. Yet in our stressful times people get caught in a cyclical deathtrap of anxiety that produces fear, which leads to depression, contributing to a weakened immune system that invites disease into the body, only to result in more stress and more fear.

The Westminister Confession says that there are two reasons we were born into this world. It says, "The chief aim of man (and woman) is to glorify God and to enjoy Him forever." Now that sounds easy enough, but so many of us miss out on our reason for existence, even in the church. Anna Marie and I go around all over the country, and even foreign countries, ministering to people in the church, and we find it is true everywhere: God's people are a mess too! We say, "You people, you are a mess! We are a mess, can we go to God now?" For some reason they just weep, and cry with us, and they say "Amen, we'll try that!" What a concept: going to God.

The beauty of the Creator God is, He came down here to join us in our brokenness. He sent Jesus to die for us, to take our sins, our sicknesses, and diseases on his own body on the cross. He did not leave us orphans, without help. He came to us because He loves us. He could not bear to see the afflictions of all the people and remain in heaven while we suffer. He bore the things that are pounding us into the ground, and He just loves it when we call out for Him to break and destroy the heavy yoke of bondage off our lives.

God's River of Mercy

Because of the uncertainty of these times and the fear that so many people are living under, there is an extraordinary need for communities of healing that house the virtue and giftedness of God for reaching out to His broken people. We are a post 9/11 culture where there are constant alerts against potential evil striking our homeland. It is the fear of the unknown that has gripped our populace. We speak to parents and their children about their excessive fears of what might be coming. Jesus said that men's hearts will fail them for fear of what is coming on the earth. We live in a desert land of spiritual lack and penury, a wilderness of wild animals and creatures of darkness. But our God is a very present help in a time of trouble. The greater the impossibility in any situation, the greater the response from God. The good news is that every place the river goes it brings life, healing, restoration, protection, and blessing. Rivers always seek out low places, and the depths to which we have plunged in the spiritual climate of our day is the very place the waters of this healing river will break forth to bring life and blessing to destroy death. This river is a real life spiritual force coming down from heaven's throne into the lives of people all around us. It flows into their real life circumstance. Sante is a prophetic sign to us, his very name cries out for wholeness and healing for all.

Obedience Precedes Faith

The second lesson of Sante's story has to do with the issue of faith. Many people have a very difficult time with the idea of faith. They believe that faith is something WE do, and it ends up becoming an exercise in mental gymnastics leading to a major cerebral drain. We try to work up faith so as to impress God, or cajole God into giving us answers to our prayers, but this is contrary to the true nature of biblical faith.

Faith is totally God based and gift centered. **"Faith comes by hearing and hearing by the word of God." Romans 10:17** Faith Comes. Faith is a pure gift. It comes when the word of God is spoken or preached under an anointing of the Holy Spirit, and the heart receives that word, for it is with the heart that a person is able to believe. The head can be informed and actively engaged in the process, but it is the heart (or the spirit of the person) that receives this gift called faith.

Bishop William Jackson Cox ordained me to the priesthood in January of 1993. He is the most Jesus I have ever seen in anyone, and his wife, Betty, is the same way. They have spoken many truths into me, but one truism that remains so strong in me is this, "Obedience sometimes precedes faith." This is what happened with Sante. When all the feelings and emotions surrounding compassion for that sick child were gone, we were left with one chief substance: obedience to God's word. We are not led by feelings, in fact, feelings can get us into a lot of trouble unless they are under the reign of the Holy Spirit. John Wimber said one time, "I can get into the supernatural a lot quicker from a rational base, than from an emotional base." I thought that was very practical of John, for

Christians can be the most rational people on the planet. But it is true, when we have nothing left, we have obedience to what the scripture tells us to do. The rest is up to God. He is the one who is responsible for the performance of and the completion of His own Words. FAITH CAME for Santes' healing after we DID the scripture. Somebody said one time that we have the gift of "showing up." How true that is. All God needs is our hands. The rest is up to Him. Doesn't that take all the pressure off of us? Faith, then, becomes a wonderful thing to delight in and not an arduous presumption. We learn not to be such busy and frustrated doers, but to become grateful, relaxed receivers. I want my whole body to become a receiver of the message of love from heaven and any giftings God wants to pour out through this vessel. God did not design us to bear the burdens of this world or of His ministry, or to make things happen for Him. He designed us to GLORIFY HIM AND TO ENJOY HIM FOREVER. Real hard! Bishop Quinn, the third bishop of the Diocese of Texas used to say, "If you don't enjoy your religion, would you please get you another one."

I would like to share one final thought on Sante. Opportunities for healing evangelism are always popping up. We have learned to look for them most anywhere. There are fine people all over our cities who need a church family around them, to love them, and to pray for their healing needs. How many people are out there in our communities that are just like this wonderful couple? They are just waiting for someone to love them, and care about them, and to invite them to go to the place where God's presence can touch them. God wants to reach them with his great compassion. And it is not hard to do.

A Childlike Faith

We have a friend named David Weidner who is a priest in the Episcopal Church, and this friend has two fine young boys. On Wednesday nights this priest holds healing services for the church he pastors, and his two little ones are in the service much of the time. Like young boys are prone to do, they color, or play, or even sleep during the proceedings, and I'm sure my friend has wondered, as one would, how much they get out of being there in the healing services. However, we know that there is a healing environment provided by the Holy Spirit, and we know that anyone who enters that place is permeated with that healing light. One day an older woman came to the church for prayers.

She had fallen in the middle of the night, and she was in such pain; she felt like she had perhaps broken her arm. She was agonizing in a prayer circle, praying with several others and waiting for her turn, when all of a sudden, one of the priest's boys broke into the room through the door, running up to the woman. He touched her on the arm (no one knew of her condition) in the exact location of the injury, and said, "Jesus heals you." Instantly, the pain left the woman's badly bruised arm. She stood there agog! How in the world did this little child know her problem; how in the world did the pain leave? She shared the story, and all were totally amazed at this, especially since it was just a child who prayed. When told, the priest ran to find his son, and asked, "Johnny, what made you do that?" This is the answer he gave, **"Daddy, I was just doing what I saw you doing."** Wow! What a profound statement! In the simplicity of a child lies the resident recipient of all the riches of God's grace. If God can use an eight-year-old little boy, perhaps he could use us too?

The Next Reformation

This response to the father's question by the son had such an impact on me that I have to say, the answer may be the basis for the next

Reformation in the Church universal. Luther shook the world with the simple statement that "salvation is by faith." The scriptures were opened up to an entire world bringing light and illumination, major revelation, and healing restoration. God sent his word to heal us. The problem is, as Alan Vincent, a missionary from Bombay, India says, "We have been cultured in an over-familiarity with a 'non-powerful Jesus.' " Even our primary healing and evangelistic ministries are overly specialized for the relatively few and not even remotely effective in reaching the masses of peoples on this planet. With all these churches, and all these programs, and all these buildings, America remains unchanged. Her children are dying in a quagmire of spiritual darkness. They are waiting for God to bare His mighty right arm, and smash their chains, and liberate them from their enslavement to addictions. All Satan hands them is:

- Death.
- Obsessive sensuality.
- Greed.
- Addictions.
- Temporary fixes to drive the stake deeper into the heart of their generation.

For the Church to make a full impact, we need a reformation of identity and practice to counter the lies of the enemy. In many ways we are, as Christians in this world, coming to know whom we are and what we are to do. We are "sons" of the Living God, and if we are "sons," then heirs to the richest treasures in heaven. We are *joint-heirs* with Christ. All Jesus has is ours; we get the same inheritance as him. What else can the title *joint-heirs* mean? The call is becoming clear and passion is heating up to get the job done. The Church of Jesus Christ is rising up to

> **... the unity of the faith and the knowledge of the Son of God, to maturity, to the measure of the full stature of Christ. We must no longer be children tossed to and fro and blown about by every wind of doctrine....**
>
> **Ephesians 4: 13-14**

As the late John Wimber, a wonderful healing evangelist used to say, "Do we get to do it now?" We have talked about "it" long enough. It's time to do it! But the doing of the works of Jesus must come out of the intimacy Jesus had with his Father in heaven. If we can receive the revelation that God is our Father, then the revelation that we are "sons" will follow. We are not beggars in the house of the Lord, we are intimate "sons" and "daughters" sharing in the Father's business. "Sons" and "daughters" go into business with their daddies. It is time to grow up, and go into business the way Jesus did. **"When we cry Abba! Father! it is that very Spirit bearing witness with our spirit that we are children of God." Romans 8:15-16**

My wife and I believe in openly using the "**E**" word even though Will Willimon, the chaplain at Duke Divinity School, said that we Episcopalians can't even say the word *evangelism*. He said that every time we try to say it, the word comes out: **Eeeeeeee-UCH –AR –IST!** Anna Marie and I teach on healing, preach it from the pulpit, and expect it to happen. The people of God are then able to respond to the spoken Word, and faith is birthed. (People will always rise to the level of preaching in their midst.) We minister that evangelism goes with healing. As some one said, "Not one New Testament church was established without signs and wonders." **Demonstrations of power and mercy, given by the Spirit of God, will do more to win this present generation than all the programs of the church combined.**

To enter our "sonship" (daughters are "sons" too, for there is no male or female in Christ Jesus) we must resolve the dilemma of faith. To come to the simplicity of faith I personally had to go through a tremendous faith crisis when I was leaving seminary in 1981. I was serving at a small student church on the north side of Tyler, Texas and commuted to school for classes during the weekdays. My last class was only for two weekends, and it was on the topic of Human Sexuality. Part of the curriculum carried us into an exercise in which we were to "take in" all kinds of pornography and sexual expressions of every kind imaginable. By the time we finished the exercise I was physically sick. It was awful! With the exposure we had to this filth we were supposed to become more aware of how human beings display their sexuality. Believe me, as a sinner before receiving the Holy Lord into my heart as savior, I had all the exposure anyone ever needs to split hell wide open. When asked to participate in a round table discussion and to share our reflections on the experience, I simply said, "I'm appalled. I came out of that stuff, and now you want me to go back?" The professor said quickly, "Next." I was so stricken with grief over the affair, and so worn out from the whole three years of study, that I hit a brick wall. I cratered. I was so discouraged that I just wanted to quit, in fact, I was seriously thinking about telling Anna Marie that I was going to resign on the following Sunday and find another career. So I packed up my car with the final load of belongings, and took off for home.

On the way I turned on the radio and searched for something to take my mind off my troubles, when I heard a loud voice coming from a woman preacher saying these words, "Oh I know you are discouraged, in fact, you want to give up don't you?" Well I had heard this Great Gospel Station of the Gulf Coast before, and frankly, some of the preaching was pretty hokey, so I reached to change the channel. I said to myself, "I'm an intellectual, I can't be listening to this." Then I heard the voice say, "Uh, uh, don't you touch that dial!" Startled, I jumped back! I got as far away from that radio as I could without climbing out the window. She said, "I know how you feel. It looks hopeless, and there just doesn't seem to be anything you can do right now, isn't that right?" I said, "Yes ma'am." Here I am talking to a radio—carrying on a conversation with a mess of wires and tubes. Dear Me! Yet somehow God was talking straight to my heart. I was undone. He really does know our very thoughts, and here He was showing up right there in my car. She said, "Now honey there is only one thing you need to do." I said through my tears, "Yes ma'am." "You need to return to God", she continued, "And do you know what? God will return to you. You don't have to give up; you just need God back in your life again. He never left, you are the one who left." She was quoting from Malachi 3:7.

I wept openly before the Lord most of the way home. I could not wait to get to my office to see if that text was really there, and sure enough it was. I read it for myself, and I vowed on my knees to "return to God, so God could return to me." I missed Him so; I missed my first love. I was so exhausted from studying God I lost Him in the process. If you were God would you want to be "studied" all day? My sermons were dry, nothing was happening in the church. It was all, dare I say it: BORING! But I said, "God how do I return to you?" Then I heard these words, inside me, down deep: "Believe me again."

Every disciple of Jesus was called to the healing ministry. When he sent out the seventy in Luke 10, he commanded them to heal the sick and say to the people, "The Kingdom of God has come near to you." He did not say that the healing ministry was separated for a special few with healing gifts. The power and anointing of the Spirit for healing belonged to the whole company. All were to enter these healing waters. Walking in these spiritual waters of Jesus is a great adventure. We can begin this adventure in faith and in what Richard Foster calls "holy naiveté." It is a kind of rational/supra-rational innocence that captivates the imagination; it is a childlike trust with a certain immediacy and enthusiasm of response. The Scripture says Jesus appeared to the eleven as they sat at table; and he upbraided them for their unbelief and hardness of heart, because they had not believed those who saw him after he had risen. And he said to them,

> **Go into all the world and preach the gospel to the whole creation. And these signs will accompany those who believe: in my name they will... lay their hands on the sick; and they will recover.**
>
> **Mark 16:15-18**

**Somewhere, Somehow, Somebody
Has Got to Start Believing
This Thing Again!**

Questions for Small Group Discussion

1. How is faith not an intellectual or cerebral activity?

2. Faith is a free gift poured out upon us by the administrations and operations of the Holy Spirit. What does it mean faith comes?

3. When does "obedience precede faith?"

4. Is there nothing so powerful as obedience?

5. What does it mean we have been cultured in unbelief?

6. Do we need another Reformation in the Church?

7. What part do the works of the Spirit and Power have with evangelism?

8. How do you respond to the fact that no New Testament church was established without signs and wonders?

CHAPTER THREE

"The Amazing Power of Forgiveness"

Third Sign

For if you forgive others their trespasses, your heavenly Father will also forgive you; but if you do not forgive others, neither will your Father forgive your trespasses.

Matthew 6: 14-15

One day a man named Jeff and his wife Vivian approached me on the streets of a small town where I was a pastor. He appeared gaunt and pale. One could tell he was seriously ill. He had heard about our church, and he asked if he could come to the meeting that night. We had an evangelist speaking in some revival services. He told me he had cancer and was given a short time to live, and had been told to get his affairs in order. I welcomed the couple with open arms. They were so beautiful!

They showed up at the church that night, and heard the evangelist deliver a powerful sermon on faith and how a bitter unforgiving heart will cancel out faith in a person's life. After hearing it, this man began to weep. I elbowed my wife and said, "Look at him, his face has color in it." Even after he stopped weeping, one could still see the color in his once ashen face. We sensed something significant had happened and that the spoken Word had brought faith into this man. He came down for healing prayer at the end of the meeting, and we anointed him with oil and prayed the prayer of faith.

While we were praying for him, he confessed murder in his heart for a partner who had stolen a large sum of money from him and had skipped town. His aim was to find his partner and kill him. His wife told me that he was full blood Cherokee Indian and he meant it. We thanked God that during that sermon God convicted him of hatred and of bitterness towards this man. He forgave the man the debt, and was free then to ask for healing. We anointed him with oil, prayed the prayer of faith, and gave praise for God's healing touch on his body, and for God removing the cancer. Later on that week he confessed to me that the real cancer he had was in his soul. He said that bitterness was the poison within him that was killing him. Shortly after this, the doctors put him in the hospital to remove a five-inch tumor in the top of his mouth with all the roots that were growing into his brain. After a biopsy on the tumor, the doctor came in with a report that it was benign. He was completely confused because he had been ninety-nine percent sure it was an aggressive form of malignant cancer. "Benign tumors do not behave like this at all," he said. The family did the dance of joy. However, the sedate doctor informed the wife of this man that he still had to go in and take out the roots that had grown into the brain cavity. He warned not to be too elated, that he was not going to be real pretty when he came up out of surgery.

Later that week they took X-rays of the cranium, and there were no (zero) roots to be found anywhere. God had removed them all. Glory! This man would go on and live for many years after this experience. He had been in church much of his life, but never knew Jesus. Jesus showed him his true heart condition, and it plunged him into the healing waters of salvation, healing, and deliverance from death.

Unforgiveness is a disease in itself, and so many people are afflicted with this blight on the soul. It is probably the chief hindrance to people receiving their healing. According to experts, eighty percent of us come from dysfunctional homes. I am still looking for the twenty percent who are functional. One major reason for the dysfunctional dynamics of families is a deep woundedness that comes from bitterness and unforgiveness. Life's many blows only heighten the pain of persons already fractured by relationships filled with the poison of acrimony and resentment.

Slaves Cannot Set Slaves Free

In 2001 I went to St. Thomas at Crookes in Sheffield, England. There I saw the most incredible sight. A thousand young people loving God, worshipping with all nine of the gifts of the Holy Spirit in operation. It was glorious! But the thing that I remember most were the words of a sermon I heard from Father Mike Breen, the Rector of the church. He said, "Slaves cannot set slaves free." How true that statement is. Someone in jail is not in any position to liberate another person behind the same bars.

It is possible that deep root bondage keeps us from expressing the fullness of the divine nature within us. We cannot be fully human, nor can we be fully God's. Oh we are going to heaven, but sometimes it is hell on earth. We will not need salvation when we get to heaven; we need it NOW!! Why? It is because slaves cannot set slaves free.

Many people do not realize that Leonardo DaVinci suffered from this disease of the soul. DaVinci was a slave to bitterness. When painting the Last Supper, DaVinci who had been seriously offended by a very dear friend of his, decided to paint the face of this former friend as the face of Judas. He so hated and despised this man that he wanted the world to see him as the most notorious and vile offender of all times. However, when it came to painting the face of Jesus, Leonardo ran into a major stumbling block. No matter what he did, or how hard he tried, he could not get the face of Jesus to turn out right. He struggled mightily with this obstacle until it became an obsession with him. Finally he cried out to God, "Why will you not give me the inspiration for the face of your Son?" The Lord replied, "Until you remove the image of your enemy off the canvas of your consciousness, you will never know the image of my Son in your life." It broke DaVinci into a thousand pieces hearing these words, and he repented.

He forgave his friend and asked God to restore a right relationship between them. Immediately after the spiritual barrier was removed, the inspiration came to paint the face of Jesus. The paint flowed freely, and as millions know, this is one of the most elegant portrayals of the intimacy of Christ with his followers to ever grace a canvas of art. It is stunning in its beauty and grace. Forgiveness is a gift of God, not born of human effort but of grace from above, and it is the loveliest image on the canvas of our souls.

The Prison of Guilt

At times one of the hardest people to forgive is oneself. This kind of guilt is a monumental stressor. It is the worst kind of slavery. My first funeral was of a man and his young daughter who were killed in an automobile accident. He and his family were driving to a picnic the day the divorce decree was effective between him and his beautiful wife. The wife and son drove up on the wreckage as they were following closely in route to the picnic site. It must have been so terrible to see her husband take his last breath. My heart broke when I heard the news. I rushed home to do the funeral, and we all managed somehow to get through the difficult ordeal of burying these two young people so loved by the community. However, during the service someone went up to the mother and said, "That's what happens to divorced people." Can you imagine the size of the knife that pierced her heart? Oh the hurts that can happen right there in God's house. (Religion does not help anyone unless Jesus has truly changed a person's heart.)

For months we watched this beautiful young woman become eaten up with guilt. She could forgive everyone else but herself. She had such a good heart, but this inner root of guilt was devastating to her. One Saturday, my wife told me to get over to her house immediately, for having talked with this woman on the phone, she sensed that something terrible might happen if someone did not intervene. I dashed to her house and found her sitting on her balcony at the brink of sanity. She looked like a frightened animal caught in a searchlight. She said to me, "I am going to run down that road and never stop screaming!" I knew she meant it, and I was scared to death. She said she had not cried in weeks, and COULD NOT cry. And me, I had not even had counseling 101 in seminary yet. I prayed the quick "Oh God, what now" prayer, and asked her to close her eyes. (God really shows up on that prayer.) I asked her to see Jesus on the cross. To my amazement, she did. I said, "Do you see the nails in his hands?" She said, "Yes." I said, "Do you see the nail in his feet?" She nodded. Then real strong, I said, "NOW YOU TELL HIM IT'S NOT ENOUGH!!" I sat back as I watched a miracle. A big tear formed in the corner of her eye, and the Hoover Dam broke. She just cried and cried and cried some more.

About that time her son came tearing up the driveway. I got up and left. Just like that! I knew God had just restored her mind to her. She, to this day, is one of our dearest friends, and I learned that morning on a balcony in the middle of the country in East Texas, that there is NOTHING JESUS' BLOOD CANNOT HEAL. HE IS ALWAYS MORE THAN ENOUGH!

Cleaning the Inside of the Cup

Unforgiveness has a devastating and detrimental effect on the inner workings of each one of us. It mars our outlook, blinds us to true friendships, and hinders our ability to relate freely and lovingly with God's creation all around them. But unforgiveness and bitterness affect our bodies as well, especially the immune system. The reason this is true is because unforgiveness and bitterness of heart are enormous stressors on the body. Stressors are known contributors to sickness and disease in the body. Dr. John Corbett is a friend of ours and a member of the Order of St. Luke the Physician. John taught on this subject in a Healing Conference we did in Boise, Idaho during the summer of 1999. He said, "As the immune system is worn down, T-cells, Killer Cells, and Cytokines are depleted, weakening the bodies' ability to fight off viruses, germs, and other invaders into our systems. This is why the healing ministry has long associated diseases like arthritis and rheumatism with the root cause of bitterness towards others." John explained that sometimes this could influence an autoimmune reaction where the body turns in on its self and begins to attack itself bringing great damage to the joints of the body. Bringing the person to forgiveness and repentance toward the person they have bitterness towards also releases healing into those joints.

Norman Cousins, who shut himself up in a motel room with tapes of the Three Stooges and Laurel and Hardy, laughed his way out of a terminal disease. Before he died in 1990, he was on staff at UCLA in the Psycho-Neuro Immunology Department. He studied the effects of laughter, faith, and hope on the bodies' ability to fight off disease. These human responses to disease or trauma were quantified by observing a defini-tive lift in the numbers of T-Cells, Killer Cells, and Cytokines over into very health producing levels.

Jesus takes healing into the deepest parts of a person's being. He gets past the externals and gets right down to the heart of the matter, and He exposes the true root issue of where problems lie. What good would it do to be completely healed on the outside and still diseased within? Some people are not healed in healing meetings because the root cause of the disease is not exposed and dealt with. God is not interested in just washing the outside of the cup; God is interested in the inside of the cup. Ezekiel's healing river of water is not natural water but spiritual water for life and blessing. This is perfectly depicted in the story of Jesus and the Samaritan woman at the well in John the fourth chapter. Jesus said to the woman at the well in **John 4:13-14, "Anyone who drinks of this water will be thirsty again, but whoever drinks of the water I give will never thirst. Indeed the water I give him will become in him a spring of water welling up to eternal life."** She thought Jesus was just trying to satisfy her natural physical needs, but Jesus went far past the physical realm and launched her out into the deep recesses of her spiritual desire. The healing occurs when spiritual eyes are opened. The people see exactly who they are and where they are in relationship to the mighty, holy, and awesome God we serve. Their true heart condition is revealed. It has been noted that many people come to meetings seeking healing, not the HEALER. What a great surprise when what they receive is so much more than the relief from physical symptoms alone. It is our job to get people to seek the HEALER. We are always astounded at the wisdom and effectiveness of His works. The greatest healing that occurs is when the healer comes into a person's heart. It is truly healing from the "inside-out."

The early stages of Ezekiel's river are offered as personal metaphors to depict the early stages of growth and development for the Christian in the seminal stages of faith. It is assumed that at some point a person must decide to step into the River. The man Jesus, standing in the midst of God's River is calling, "Come on in, the water is fine." He calls us forth into the waters, but God is good and so tender; he does not ask us to swim right away. He knows our fear of the water (for we really do fear the unknown in this situation), and he will never ask us to do more than we are ready for. God is the great encourager. He wants us where he is; he is calling us forth.

Stepping into the River

One of the greatest obstructions to people receiving their healing is that people just want to live their lives as they please, but go to heaven. Charles Simpson was my favorite preacher in my mid-twenties, and during the mid 1970s. I learned so much from him. He was funny, bright, gifted, and fiery! He had a visitation from God in his Baptist Church. (God started moving everywhere in those days.) He had a man in his church who was always saying, "I just want to make the gate." Charles tried to convince him that there was so much more to a life with Jesus than just escaping hell. One night the Spirit of God came powerfully on their church and people were under a strong anointing to repent, and to be filled with the Holy Spirit. Many were down at the altar rail weeping and calling out to God. Charles happened to notice this man, over in the corner of the altar weeping and muttering some prayer Charles couldn't hear. He was so fascinated at the sight, the pastor eased over to get a closer take on what was happening. As he got to where he could hear the words he was saying in the most precious tones, "I made the gate, I made the gate."

God knows it is time for people to enter the healing waters. Statistics say that approximately fifty percent of people in the church are not sure of their salvation. It is no wonder there is so much sickness in the church. We have been exhorted by the Apostle Paul to be TRANSFORMED and not to conform to the thinking and behavior of this present world. This is to be a decisive moment with a decisive experience. Either we are transformed into a new creature or we are not. The word is *metamorphoo* in the Greek language. It is where we get our word "metamorphosis." The image is of being a caterpillar one moment and then, in a complete change of creature, a butterfly the next.

The Truth Shall Make You Free

How long will God's people remain in the shallow waters of ignorance, deprivation, and apathy in a spirituality of poverty and paucity? These are terrible barriers to God's blessings, and costly in price. This dreadful fact came home to Anna Marie one night in Longview, Texas. My wife saw an eighty-year-old man come to Christ in a Terry Fulham meeting in Longview. This man had been in church all his life, but when God's plan of salvation was clearly displayed in Terry's message, this man knew he had to transact business with God. He prayed to receive Christ right there in front of God and all the people. He stood and cried as he asked a simple question, "Why, Fr. Fulham? Why didn't anyone ever tell me about this before?" My wife wept, as did so many, at how beautiful this sacred moment was. Part of it may have been the pain of realization that the church often does not even know the One who wants to bring us to a face-to-face encounter with himself and the reality of the spiritual world in which he dwells forever. This was the experience of the man in Longview. He had been in church all his life. However, in one powerful meeting his life was totally transformed. He had just enough religion to keep him from deeper encounters with God's Healing River. The water seemed good, and God gave him all the freedom in the world to remain the same. It seemed like it was enough to just be in church, and it seemed like the right thing to do. However, one powerful and clear biblical sermon gave this man the experience one only dreams of. It was so heavenly. He stood immediately, like a child, and received the blessing of God. He had entered the kingdom of God with all its vast treasures.

Jesus Christ came into this world to help people just like you and just like me. The word is *sodzo* in the Greek language. It has such a rich meaning. It does not just mean "making heaven." It means more than immunity from the fire of judgment for sin and rebellion against God and his laws. It is, perhaps, the richest word in all human languages. It means to save, to protect, to preserve, to heal, to deliver from evil or harm, and to provide with total abundance. After Jesus bought our salvation on Calvary's cross, and ascended into heaven to ever intercede for us, He did not leave us desolate; He laid out a lavish banquet. He does not begrudge us one blessing, but longs to see us come into the riches of Christ, and to eat at his table of heavenly blessing. Truly, whatever the obstruction may be to receiving these blessings, God wants to deal with it, and free his people to enjoy his life to the uttermost.

Questions for Small Group Discussion

1. Discuss the relationship between Spirit, Soul, and Body. How does one affect the other?

2. Why is it so hard to forgive the ones who offend us?

3. Can unforgiveness cancel one's faith?

4. How do bitter roots down inside a person manifest outwardly in terms of behaviors and actions?

5. Can we successfully hide or cover up these inner roots of bondage?

6. Are you free to live in the full blessings of Salvation?

7. Is it truly possible to live as "freed persons" without bondage?

8. Is the modern liberation from our "puritanical roots" getting rid of guilt?

CHAPTER FOUR

"The Healing Presence"

Fourth Sign

As the deer pants for streams of water, so my soul pants for you, O God. My soul thirsts for God, for the living God. When can I go and meet with God?

Psalm 42:1-2

The key to the healing ministry is "presence." Meeting WITH God in his manifest present form is the most vital part of what we do in healing prayer. Presence is the number one factor in how effective healing conferences and missions are. To the degree that the presence of God is asked for, anticipated, acknowledged, and appreciated, one can calculate how effective healing prayer is going to be.

Alan and Eileen Vincent are spiritual parents, mentors, and friends. They were missionaries in Bombay for thirty years. They have greatly impacted our lives and the lives of so many people we love. Our lives sometimes cross paths in ministry, and in one such instance we experienced a most extraordinary anointing in a healing mission.

Many years ago, a slaughter of Indians took place on the site of what is now called Comanche Hill. That site on the north side of San Antonio had been a magnet for adherents of the New Age, who went there for harmonic convergence, and for Satanists from around the city who found it fertile ground for sacrifice because of the blood that cried out for vengence from that desecrated ground. The Lord told Alan to get a good bottle of wine and to consecrate it to the Lord for communion. They prayed over the bottle that Alan bought, had communion, and then poured the rest of the wine on the ground, claiming it back in the name of the Lord Jesus, and setting apart that site for holy purposes.

Right down from Comanche Hill sits a wonderful church. About the same time this spiritual cleansing took place, this church began to stir to new life, and I do not believe this is a coincidence. A group of people there became very interested in starting a healing ministry at the church. Their fine priest came on board with the idea and we all decided to do a first ever Healing Mission at the church. On the first day of the Mission the music was absolutely awesome. The church had hired a band that was well accustomed to "letting the stops out," and the presence of God was very strong! People came from other parts of the city, but for the most part the participants were comprised of the members of the church. Words of knowledge began to flow freely like we had never seen before, and the Lord began to heal people all over the sanctuary. The leadership in their healing ministry informed us that somewhere around twenty notable and undeniable miracles took place in that weekend.

The most memorable miracle took place on Sunday morning and may go down as the most remarkable healing we've ever witnessed. A woman who contracted Polio when she was eleven years old attended that church. She walked on crutches, the kind of crutches that have those heavy arm braces. Never have I seen a more angelic face. Everyone who meets this woman loves her. This particular day was her day—an appointment with God.

I preached on God revealing the Father to us, and I told of the unfailing love of our Father. At the communion rail, she stood propped up by her crutches. I just reached up in one of those moments where every movement, even every glance, is a prayer and I touched her on the side of her head praying, "Father, will you let this bread be healing to your daughter today?" I went on down the communion rail after placing the bread in her hand.

When this woman got back to her pew, she lost it. She was in the real presence of God. There is no other way to say it. She wept profusely as she forgave her own physical father who simply was not there for her when she had such desperate needs as a little girl. Her forgiveness became an open door for the Holy Spirit to act, and He, the Holy Spirit of God, said to her, "Receive your healing." It was as clear as a bell.

When leaving the church, her radiant face shining, she said to the priest and me as we stood at the back of the church, "I've been to *church* today." "Yes you have," we said, "we all have." When she got home she was still in the presence of the Lord, and incredibly, the pain was leaving her joints. She told us later, that as she made lunch, she began to feel better and better, when to her utter amazement, she walked right out of those crutches! One can only imagine the dancing and the jubilation in that home. AND, one can only imagine the shock when she walked into her office building the next day, and negotiated stairs for the first time since age eleven without any assistance at all. I'd give a hundred dollars to have seen the looks on the faces of her cohorts. Don't you know they had to have asked "WHERE does she go to church?"

God is so full of surprises. He does the most marvelous things for believing people. One minister from Great Britain spoke to us many years ago about the renewal that had come to the Anglican Church. He said of his home, "God is doing surprising things, with surprising people, at surprising times, in surprising places; don't be surprised." However, it has become surprisingly predictable how God manifests his presence when the worship preparation and the prayer preparation are firmly established as integral parts of a healing event. The greatest times we have in the healing ministry are when the presence of God is strong, the worship is the most dynamic, and the prayers are the most focused. The presence is a tangible atmosphere in the meetings. That weekend in the church at the foot of Comanche Hill is forever etched in our memories as totally miraculous and charged with divine favor and power. The ground is crying out better things than we can ever imagine.

The Fourth Voice

We have dear friends named Jim and Sharon Austin. Jim was a first chair trumpet player for the Houston Symphony for years. At one time he was considered one of the top five trumpet players in the country. He was and still is a professor of music at the University of Houston. I have never known anyone like Jim. He can be sitting at a railroad crossing bar, hear the horn blow from the engineer, and call out, "B Flat." He has perfect pitch.

Jim told me something that really stirred my spirit. He said that there is a phenomenon in music called the "fourth voice." On one occasion, during a Houston Symphony rehearsal, the conductor called for Jim and the other two trumpet players to play the opening part to the piece they were working on. They fired up, and something incredible happened. The first chord itself was so perfectly in tune, and they were in such perfect pitch together, that the conductor heard a fourth instrument. He stopped the three trumpets and said, "Beginning," in order to start them up a second time. Again, he heard the fourth instrument. "Gentlemen, please, only the trumpets," he said after stopping them again. Technically, the three horns were is such harmony that they picked up the fundamental note, or the A below, and it created another sound so distinct that the conductor actually thought another instrument was playing. The chord was so finely tuned to a certain vibration that it set off the "fourth voice."

This is a highly unusual occurrence, but it took place another time when the orchestra was tuning up. When orchestras tune up before a concert, they tune to the oboe. As the oboist began, the trumpets chimed in. They achieved this perfect pitch again, and they kept hearing an extra oboe, but only one oboe was playing.

It turned out that a tuning fork for oboes was going off in the oboist's bag. The bag was closed, but the brass section had played that note and it was so in tune with that fork that it set it off and it was really loud like someone had struck it. It is a bar two and one-half feet long, and it has a kind of spring that thumps the bar and makes the sound. It was very loud. The conductor looked rather non-plussed, as he could not figure out how he had an extra oboe. This is extremely rare, but what an experience! The horns were so in tune together that it set off the tuning device. The "fourth voice" occurs when players are in perfect pitch together.

Jesus said, **"If any two or three of you shall agree as touching anything on this earth, it shall be done for you in heaven."** **Matthew 18:19** The "fourth voice" is an allegorical illustration of a profound truth. It is an example from the physical world of what can happen when Christians get into harmony and practice the resonance of the spirit. The word in the Greek language is *sumphoneo*. It means to agree, or to be harmonious. It also means to resonate with, or to make the same sound as. There are times when crystal glasses in a room will resonate with the same sound being produced by a musical instrument or a human voice. They will produce the same sound and be in "agreement" with each other in perfect pitch. This is how an opera singer can break a crystal glass with one note.

It is the desire of God that we resonate with heaven and make the same sound as the music of heaven so that what people feel, hear, and experience is the "fourth voice" of God. This is so that we may resonate with each other and come into harmony with God for his healing ministry in the earth today. It is time for us to get into agreement with heaven—to make the same sound as heaven. God himself will sing, dance, and make music with us.

Signs of the Presence

This agreement or resonance with heaven has distinctive qualities that can be openly discerned. We have been in meetings where the air was charged with excitement and anticipation. We have been in that rarefied air of heaven where the fourth voice of God resonates in everyone present. On the other hand, we have been in places where the environment for ministry was heavy, oppressive, and burdensome. But how can we tell when the presence of God is with us, when the Holy Spirit desires to manifest Himself to us? I have developed a criterion that can be used to quantify and qualify how to measure the presence of God in worship services where ministry takes place, and how to properly discern the presence. It can be used in any type of event that involves the Holy Spirit.

First, there is what we call **Clarity.** When the Word of God is clear and penetrating in spoken form, prayer form, or sung form, then you know it is the presence of the Lord, and He is making the communication easy.

> **Indeed, the word of God is living and active, sharper than any two-edged sword, piercing until it divides soul from spirit, joints from marrow, it is able to judge the thoughts and intentions of the heart.**
>
> **Hebrews 4: 12-13**

Ideas and concepts come forth in a smooth flow of delivery, and the ears of the listener are keenly attuned to what is being said. It is as though the tongue and the ears are anointed, and there is lucidity and precise intelligibility to the thoughts being presented. A real miracle of CLARITY occurred on the day of Pentecost as a perfect example of how words were spoken, even in many tongues, and all the people understood exactly what was being said. The sower (Jesus) sows the word but in this environment it goes into the best and most fertile soil. It becomes truth that sets the person free. People behold themselves as in a clear mirror and become transformed, even taken to a new level of God's glory (2 Corinthians 3:17-18). Satan hates it when the Word becomes alive and penetrates the deepest parts of the people's being and divides the truth from lies, exposes wrong motives, thoughts, and actions.

Secondly, there is something called **Cleanness.** When the Holy Spirit is manifesting strongly there is "cleanness" in the environment with very little spiritual pollution from the enemy in the air. One can sense that Holy God is pleased to dwell in that place, and there is an overriding sense of holiness, that the event is "set apart" for God's purposes. It does not mean that everyone or everything on site has to be pure; it just means God has covered everything in His Holy Light and designated it as His own. In "prayed through" events God will take ascendancy over anything not holy in or near His Presence. One can sense in most churches that the sanctuary is a very holy room. Usually, it is prayer and anointing with oil that prepare a room for this kind of phenomenon. Some places are actually spiritually unclean, and they need a real spiritual cleansing before the anointing of God can flow freely.

Thirdly, there is another factor called **Brightness.** God is light and in Him there is no darkness at all. When God is in the room there is a certain luminescent quality. Light shines from the faces of the people, and the air is illuminated with a shiny essence that is clearly discernible. There is even brightness in people's eyes. One time Anna Marie and I were sitting in the front pew of a church that God was visiting with His presence. When the two ushers called us up to go to the altar rail for communion, we were flabbergasted by what we saw. We could see fire in the eyes of these two ushers. It brought home to us how it was said of the disciples on the day of Pentecost that people could see tongues of fire over the tops of their heads. This was the same phenomenon. Physically, it is hard to describe, but their eyes were "on fire." There is no doubt that brightness is a clear luminous aspect of the nearness of God as his people draw close to Him.

The last quality is **Joy**. A desert Father said once, "The unmistakable sign of God's presence is JOY. **"For the kingdom of God is not food and drink but righteousness, peace, and joy in the Holy Spirit." Romans 14:17** When the Lord is present, He will destroy the yoke of heaviness that burdens people. In Isaiah sixty-one it says,

> **The Lord has anointed me; he has sent me to bring good news... to provide for those who mourn in Zion (that is the church) to give them a garland instead of ashes, the oil of gladness**

instead of mourning, and the mantle of praise instead of a faint spirit.

Isaiah 61:1

This is more than an emotion of temporary happiness. It is an anointing for Joy, the oil of *gladness*. It is a spiritual substance and a spiritual force in the life of the believer. This kind of joy comes from the nearness of God. He will take the ashes of all our broken and ravaged dreams and replace them with victory. We will put on a spiritual garland, our symbol of triumph and exultation. Oh the joy that comes from being with God! When these things are all in place, you can know God is sitting enthroned on the praises of His people, and He is about to pour out blessings that cannot be contained. Without this recognition, acknowledgment, and anticipation, we really do miss out on a great deal of excitement and joy.

God gives us a sure fire way of telling what is of Him and what is not. This is becoming more important than ever before with all the deception and craftiness of the evil one that is in the world at this time. When the anointing is strong with God's presence the factors that I have mentioned are present, anything that is NOT of God sticks out like a sore thumb.

One time we were in a meeting with the Tribe of Judah, a biker group that rides Harleys and preaches the Gospel. A band was there really cooking in the Spirit, and the anointing was at about an eight on a scale of one to ten. At a pause in the music, a man stood up and began to "prophesy." The only problem was, the longer he talked, the lower the anointing measure dipped. It dropped quickly to a five, then a four. The meeting was just about over anyway, so its premature ending was not all that noticeable, but I had had enough. I stood up and abruptly ended the meeting. Afterwards, the head of the Tribe of Judah came up to me and asked, "Would you get name tags for tomorrow so I can tell who is real and who is not?" In other words, he knew something was out of whack, too. It turned out that the man who was prophesying was a leader of a small group of people who lived together, and the man was sleeping with about four women besides his wife.

Our God insists on keeping it Clean, Bright, and Clear so the true joy of Jesus can flow, and we can stay out of a lot of trouble. Psalm 91 says that God will put us under his wings (presence) and will become our refuge and our protection from all evil. Thank God for the gift of the discerning of spirits, and that we can see, hear, and touch the holy presence. Thank God that we can live, and move, and have our being in, and experience the atmosphere of, heaven. It is where we belong, and God has made a way for us to live in His presence while here in this darkened world of sin and pain.

God Misses Us

Presence is the very thing Adam and Eve lost in their fall from grace in the Garden of Eden,

So the Lord God banished him from the Garden of Eden to work the ground from which he had been taken. After He drove the man out, He placed on the east side of the Garden of Eden cherubim and a flaming sword flashing back and forth to guard the way to the tree of life

Genesis 3:23-24

God misses us! He longs for our company and for our companionship. In the beginning,

They heard the sound of the Lord God walking in the garden at the time of the evening breeze, and the man and his wife hid themselves from the

presence of the Lord God among the trees of the garden. But the Lord God called to the man, and said to him, 'Where are you?' He said, 'I heard the sound of you in the garden, and I was afraid, because I was naked; and I hid myself.

Genesis 3: 8-10

God is still calling for us today, "Where are you?" He misses us. He knows we have gotten so caught up in the difficulties and trials of everyday living. We have pursued other things besides Him. We are so distracted by the materialism and sensuality of "this present darkness" that we have almost completely forgotten God. Yet we hide naked and vulnerable to the harsh changes and uncertainties of life, and we remain in our fears. God is saying, "Come out from your hiding places, come back to my care and to the refreshing cool of the day as we commune together again. Come back home to the safety and refuge of my protection. I love you and I miss you. Won't you please come back home to me? I will cover you and protect you; I will shield you and take away all your fears. I never designed life to be this harsh for you. I want you back in my care."

You who live in the shelter of the Most High (His Presence), who abide in the shadow of the Almighty, will say to the Lord, "My refuge and my fortress; my God in whom I trust." For He will deliver you from the snare of the fowler and from the deadly pestilence; He will cover you with his pinions, and under his wings you will find refuge; his faithfulness is a shield and buckler. You will not fear the terror of the night or the arrow that flies by day, or the pestilence that stalks in the darkness, or the destruction that wastes at noonday.

Psalm 91:1-6

Healing Presence Unifies

Several years ago in a healing conference held in a hotel ballroom in Pueblo, Colorado, a large group of non-denominational people came together with some denominational people. It was quite a challenge because the two cultures were as opposite as they could be. One group was accustomed to quiet, reflective worship, and the other group was used to loud, boisterous, and highly demonstrative worship. The room was charged with energy and yet there was a sense of tension in the air too. There is nothing wrong with either style of worship, but the real kicker is getting them together to see Jesus work. Jesus is contemplative, charismatic, born-again and liberal (progressive) all wrapped up in one complete expression of the wonder of God. I joked that one group was like a rally at a football game and the other group like a pork roast at a Kosher wedding, which is my way of dealing with discomfort. Most laughed along with me.

At one point a woman absolutely came unglued. She was very angry with all of the distractions and all the noise. Someone would say "Amen," and she would just cringe. At one of our breaks, she sat with me and asked, "I'm mean, aren't I?" I said, smiling, "Yes ma'am, you're a junkyard dog," thinking she was kidding. But she meant it! She said, "I just hate it when people say, 'Amen!'" I felt so bad that she and others were unhappy. Jesus loved all of us, but I had no idea how God was going to solve the problem of unity.

That night, when we prayed for the sick, a beautiful little nine-year-old blonde girl with freckles came up for ministry. She touched her right ear and said, "I'm deaf in this ear and eighty percent deaf in my left ear, and it is going real fast. Is there anything you can do for me?" Have you ever had your heart just melt on the spot? The whole room let out a collective groan. Tears began to flow from denominational eyes and non-denominational eyes. It just did not matter anymore who carried what label. All we knew was that God "showed up" in a big way with the most extraordinary anointing for compassion. It was as thick as the smoke in that room. We begged God to heal her out of the very groanings of the Spirit Himself.

I checked her hearing after praying for a while, but nothing seemed to happen. So we prayed some more, and again, nothing happened. I told her we believed in soaking prayer and that she should come back again the next time we had prayers for healing. We went on to the next person, a man with a bad back, and God touched him and healed him.

That night in the hotel room, I had words with God. You have to be real humble to have words with God like that, but after all, I had read Alex McCollough's book, *Humility and How I Achieved It,* so it was all right. (Alex is a wonderful bishop in a denomination up in New York State.) I said, "God why didn't you heal that precious little girl, and then turn around and heal the man? You saw how much compassion there was in that room." He did not answer me one word. As a friend of mine said one time, "How fortunate God is to have you."

The next day right before the first morning session, she walked into the ballroom. There was a ruckus that caused us all to look up, and it was the "denominationals." They were jumping up and down acting just like the "other guys." The little girl had gotten up at 8:00 A.M. completely healed. She was one hundred percent well in both ears. It was a miracle of New Testament proportions, and we all became one, which may have been another New Testament miracle!

On Sunday, at what could now be truly called the NON-DENOMINATIONAL CHURCH, the woman I jokingly called "a junkyard dog" sat on the front row with me, got filled with the Holy Spirit, and danced with me all over the front of the sanctuary! She had hung around the banks of the River of God just long enough to fall in! She jumped into that river and began to splash around. She sang heartily, she raised her hands, and God baptized this dear, precious woman in His Holy Glorious River of Living Water. And guess what? She BECAME a RIVER! She was already a total blessing and a sincere and wonderful Christian, but that day she went to the spout where the glory comes out! I laughed with her until I was blue. What joy! What a wonderful Lord we serve! Her life and her ministry would never be the same again.

Are you thirsty for more? Is yours a dry and lonely world? The world's solutions just don't work! Go to Jesus. He does not just give you a trickle of blessing, but he gives you a river that never runs dry. This is it:

> **And wherever the river goes every living creature which swarms will live and there will be very many fish, for this water goes there, that the waters of the sea may become fresh; so everything will live where the river goes."**
>
> **Ezekiel 47:9**

May I invite you to step out of the endless quest to satisfy your soul's thirst, that quest that leads from one spiritual fad to the next? Spiritual fads may feel good temporarily, but they merely cover up a thirst that can only be satisfied by going deeper with Jesus. Listen as He calls you to the next level. Hear His voice say, "Come out deeper." Come out and let Jesus inundate you with his glory and power and submerge you in the place of prayer, the place of fellowship with the Lord, and the place of communion where God delights to pour out his gifts. In His Presence is the Fullness of Joy. Remember, the deeper one goes, the less is seen of that person and the more of God's Healing River our world around us receives. Then, we get to be the vessel; we get to "Be" the river. Jesus said, **"... out of his belly shall flow rivers of Living Water." John 7:38** God is calling us into the river. Jesus is the man Ezekiel saw. He is standing in the midst of the waters beckoning us to join Him. He will walk us out into the water where we are destined for the deep things of God's Healing River in our time. He wants us to get used to the water as our new habitat for existence: a life in the Spirit. Life is in His presence.

Use the Well

Agnes Sanford compared God's healing power with water. She had an old well that was more than a hundred years old. The water was delicious, soft and sweet. She had not used the well in some time, and after a power failure that disabled her modern water pump, she had occasion to tap that old well with a bucket. She tied it to a rope, and lowered the bucket only to find that there was no water, only mud in the bottom of that well. She asked a plumber friend, "Austin, what happened to my old well? There's no water in it!"

"You haven't been using it, have you?" said Austin. "When you don't use it, the well gets all clogged up with its own silt. The more you use it, the more the water comes. And as it comes it tends to come clean." The Church has not used the well of salvation very much at all in our generation. It is time to crank up the pump and get the well flowing again. It is time to "use the well." Better yet, it is time to jump in the **RIVER**.

Nobody embodied the healing presence of Jesus like Agnes Sanford. She used to minister to people in her office in her basement. Whenever someone would walk into her office, they were not walking into her presence, but into God's presence because that is where that woman chose to live. It was the healing presence that brought miracles to those she prayed for. The exciting thing is that anyone can live in that same place. It is the natural habitat for those of us who are born of the Spirit. When prayer gets dry and nothing is happening, go to the river and jump in.

A person can live in the presence all the time. Sin is the only thing that can cause it to wane, but that is why we have been given the gift of repentance. Just be a quick "repenter" and stay "fessed up." It helps greatly to keep praise music going in your home and office. We will then find the luminous and clarifying light of Jesus will protect and preserve you in ways we never imagined. It is the presence of God that brings salvation. What do you think Daniel had as his protection when he was thrown into the lion's den? Was it the armies of Israel, or some physical prowess Daniel possessed? Was it human ingenuity or his skills in animal husbandry? No, it was the presence of the Lord all over him. If one of those lions would have taken a bite out of Daniel, he would have fried like a bug being zapped by one of those blue lights.

The presence will lift you up into the heavenly realm. The Bible has many references to eagles. They are used as metaphors of our Christian walk and practice. One thing I have learned is that eagles were created for the sky. They were not created to dwell in the shadows of the earth, but to soar in the heavenlies. So were we created to soar in the heavenlies, and to obtain our blessings in "heavenly places." "Blessed be the God and Father of our Lord Jesus Christ, who has blessed us in Christ with every spiritual blessing in the heavenly places...." As one old preacher used to say, "You've got to get into the Spirit to get your blessings; it's our natural habitat." There is where we were created to live.

Let me encourage you, the healing ministry is not rocket science. We can enter this ministry at any level. It is simply the power of the love of God that directly influences the outcomes of human circumstance. It is God who intervenes in the pain, hurts, and wounds of suffering people. It is a matter of staying in the presence of God through worship, prayer, and intimacy. The healing environment around you, filled with the fragrance of Christ, will either draw people to you for God to heal, or will send you forth into some divine appointment where the very presence of God will permeate the works of darkness that keep people in bondage.

It is no wonder Moses said this after being confronted with the prospect of leaving Egypt,

If your Presence does not go with us, do not send us up from here. How will anyone know that you are pleased with me and with your people unless you go with us? What else will distinguish me and your people from all the other people on the face of the earth?

Exodus 33:15-16

Questions For Small Group Discussion

1. Is Praise just for Sunday mornings?

2. What does it mean that God's presence heals?

3. How important are peace, joy, and serenity to a healing team?

4. How can we cultivate a lifestyle of "living in the presence?"

5. What impact would it have on our worship services if the various streams of believers saturated in individual "presence" poured into the sanctuary and made a "river" of praise?

6. Does the spiritual environment of a place affect the operations and administrations of the gifts of the Holy Spirit?

7. Can we live into the presence of God on a daily basis?

8. Can you envision a "swimming in-over-our-heads" experience of worship where ALL the gifts of the Holy Spirit operate at one time?

CHAPTER FIVE

"The Same Power that Raised Jesus"

Fifth Sign

If the Spirit of him who raised Jesus from the dead dwells in you, he who raised Christ from the dead will give life to your mortal bodies also through his Spirit that dwells in you.

Romans 8:11

I received a call one morning at my brand new church. I had only been a priest there for about three months, and I wanted to do well. I also did not want to make any waves by being overly enthusiastic. Somebody asked if they thought Charismatics would make the gate. They said, "Yes, if they do not run past it." Well, I did not want to run past what God was doing, so I was going very slow in presenting the gifts of the Spirit. I figured in about a year or two, I would introduce the subject. But I got a call from some very dear prayer people who informed me of a serious tragedy. A little six-month-old child died of SIDS (Sudden Infant Death Syndrome). His dad came home from work to find him completely blue in the face. The baby sitter thought he was sound asleep. Frantically, the father rushed the child to the emergency room at a nearby hospital where he was resuscitated. One doctor said that he thought the little one had been dead for somewhere between thirty to forty minutes.

When I got to the hospital I walked into a room that had been filled with prayer. The parents and grandparents had been praying all night. There was just a blank stare on the face of their precious child, and the prognosis was very bleak. It looked like he could be in a vegetative state for the remainder of his life. The nurses and doctors, thinking the baby might have contracted meningitis, came in to draw fluids for testing. As they slid a long needle into his spinal cord, the child's eyes just continued to stare ahead with no sign of life within them. That baby gave no indication of feeling the needle at all. The prognosis did not look good.

Anna Marie and I lost a child, a beautiful and bright baby boy. Our Stephen died of Leukemia at the age of eight, so I could feel the agony in that room. When I asked if I could pray, I absolutely lost it. I sobbed and wept over their baby so intensely that one of the grandmothers felt compelled to comfort ME. She patted me on the back and finally, she said, "Can I talk to you outside?" I gained a little composure, and we stepped outside the door. She said, "Oh, Father Jack, we are so glad that you have come to pray for us." All of a sudden, we heard, "Waaaaaaaa!" Stunned, we looked at each other in amazement, then darted into the room to see a miraculous sight. That little one was fighting mad! He was hungry, and he wanted momma "right now." The baby was alert and showing no signs of coma or brain trauma whatsoever.

The doctors ran tests for several hours and found nothing wrong. Nothing! They dismissed the child to go home that afternoon. Praises to our glorious Lord! The scripture says that the **SAME power that had raised Jesus from the dead shall quicken your mortal bodies.** The word "quicken" is archaic, but the text means that power shall enter into our mortal bodies when we need it for healing, or deliverance, or any kind of provision. It was completely obvious to all of us that power had gone into the boy who had died of SIDS. Nothing else could explain the suddenness of his recovery.

Resurrection Power Falls

This same power was poured out another time in 1986 when I decided to leave a church where I was pastor. I was very discouraged; my son had just died, and I was going back to Houston to get out of debt from all the hospital bills. At this very low point in my life, God came in a very unusual display of his might. Why he would choose to use me has always been a mystery, but this was unique.

Anna Marie worked with a woman at the dental office where she was one of the hygienists, and this woman called on the day I resigned from the church. I was packing my books and loading up the truck to leave, when Anna Marie said, "Jack, Dorothy wants us to come over. Her uncle is dying, and she is afraid he is going to hell." I said, "No, I am in no place to pray for anyone who is dying. No, NO, No!" Well, she gave me that look, if you know what I mean. She batted those eyes, and it was all over for me. I said, "Alright, I'll go, but NOTHING will happen." I was truly God's man of faith and power at that moment. Sure!

When we got there, Anna Marie decided to stay in the living room to pray for ME as well as Bill, the uncle. I walked into a guest room and saw a hospital bed with a little old man lying there battered and bruised from a beating he took when he antagonized a fellow resident of his nursing home. The man beat him with his cane, and they sent him to his niece's home to die. Dorothy would get up in the middle of the night over and over because she was afraid he was slipping off into hell. Many people today do not believe in hell, but you try convincing Bill's niece of that. She knew what she saw in her uncle—the torment and the pain of his inner being. No one liked this man, not even his own family. He was mean and bitter, and he alienated himself from everyone he met.

I was a wreck. As I walked up to him in his bed he grew very restless. I said, "Bill, I've come to pray for you." He went into a rage, tearing at the sheets, and gasping for air. It turned out that his wife was an old-time Pentecostal who used to browbeat him with the Bible all the time. He hated religion and he hated preachers! Great! I was about to be the cause of killing this man with an act of prayer I did not even want to give. I said, "Now Bill, I know you have gotten a lot of religion

before, but I did not come to give you religion;
I came to give you Jesus." He fought me again
violently! (I wanted to jump out of the
window.) So I said, "Alright, alright! Let me
just pray for you, no more talk. Let's just pray!"
I put my hands on his bald head and prayed,
"Lord, this man has been exposed to all kinds
of religion, but would you just give him your
love?" And then I said something very strange.
I said, **"Besides, devil, you're not big
enough."**

Wonderfully, a big tear formed in one of Bill's
eyes. I said to myself, "That is a good sign." Dorothy and another niece had their hands on Bill's
shoulders, trying to calm him down. Praying, I
had one hand on his right arm. Suddenly, about
fifty thousand volts of power fell on Bill, cover-
ing his whole body like a blanket. It was tangible, forceful, real voltage. It ran up my arms,
and up the arms of his nieces. They jumped
back screaming, **"He got it, He got it!!"** Those
women danced all over that room. What an answer to prayer!

That night Dorothy kept getting up again
in the middle of the night, but this time it
was not for the noise of torment, but because
of the silence. She said he was so peaceful
and had the sweetest little grin on his face

all night long. He was so still she wanted to see if he was still breathing. And so it was all night, until he slipped away into eternity about 6:00 A.M., into the arms of the One who saved him.

This was a wonderful testament to the ability of prayer to move God in very difficult situations, impossible to men, but never impossible to him. Prayer links us to the power of God and even has the capability of turning reluctant, stubborn, and unwilling preachers into instruments of salvation and healing in spite of themselves. He has the power to change the greatest long shots into victories.

It was the same power that RAISED JESUS FROM THE DEAD. It's what Jesus meant when he said, **"You shall receive power when the Holy Spirit has come upon you...." Acts 1:8** It is also what is meant when it says in the Bible that virtue went forth from Jesus when the woman with the issue of blood broke through the crowd and touched the hem of Jesus' garment. **"And Jesus, perceiving** in himself that power had gone forth from him, immediately turned about **in the crowd, and said, 'Who touched my garments?'" Mark 5:30-31** Later, I compared notes with Anna Marie who told me, "I prayed the strangest prayer while I was interceding for you guys in the living room. I prayed, 'Devil, you're not big enough to hold this man.'" My, my, what kind of a wonderful God do we serve?

Palpable Voltage

The power that ministered to Bill, and sent his nieces dancing, is palpable and experiential. There have been several times in my life when the surge of this current was so great it almost knocked me to the ground. It almost knocked Milton Green, a Baptist evangelist, and me to the floor at Bedford United Methodist Church one morning in a healing conference. We just met in the hallway near the bookstore in the basement, and as we approached each other, an electrical current so strong hit us both. I, to this day, do not know what that was all about. Was it for him or for me? We were so bewildered and dazed by it, that we just walked away from it without saying a word. It may have been that one of us was healed of something or delivered of something. We won't know about it until we meet with our maker and review all the tapes of our lives. But one thing is certain, it was tangible and it was real live power.

Another place in the scriptures that points to a manifestation of this kind of power is in John's account of the arrest of Jesus in a garden near the Kidron valley. Judas brought a detachment of soldiers to arrest Jesus. Jesus asked them,

Whom are you looking for? They answered, "Jesus of Nazareth." Jesus replied, "I am He." ... When Jesus said to them, "I am He," they stepped back and fell to the ground. John 18:4-6

What kind of power is it that physically knocks a whole detachment of soldiers to the ground without Jesus lifting one finger?

The only thing I can compare this kind of experience to is when I was a carpenter's apprentice in 1972 and I accidentally sawed an electric wire in half with a buzz saw. The voltage literally drove my body to the ground. God's power is like that. It is awesome. It destroys the works of the evil one, and it is available to the church today.

Power Against Attacks

We need this power, in fact, we had better have this power flowing in our midst or some of us are not going to make it. Our enemy is very real too, and mean. The devil is determined to take us out especially if we are resisting evil. Somebody said, "If you don't run into the devil, it is a good sign you and he are going in the same direction." He hates God; he hates you and me, and he will do everything he can to get us off track.

Recently I was hit with a disease in my liver. I had jaundice, and my eyes and skin became yellow. I was so weak that I could not get out of bed, and I had tremendous pain in my abdomen on through to my back. All of this happened during a very busy schedule of healing meetings and intense ministry. I did not know how I was going to keep up with the demands. After fasting for several days, and praying for several weeks, the power of God showed up on a Saturday morning of one of our Healing Missions. It hit me while I was speaking and shook me all over the front of the sanctuary causing me to dance and shout and prophesy. I have never behaved in such a manner in CHURCH! Several of my friends thought, "Not in church, oh no, not here!" But I saw pipes sticking out of the whole front of my body sucking the very life out of me, and in my mind's eye I could see God violently blowing every one of those life-sucking pipes out of my body. All the pain left. All weakness left, and all jaundice left too. I have never had another symptom like that since.

The question I asked myself after that experience was this, **"How in the world do church**

folks make it without the power of the Holy Spirit?" The answer is, we cannot. If we get under attack, we will stay sick, or beaten down, or defeated, unless we are given access to the marvelous power that is available to us in the mighty name of Jesus Christ. He constantly went about doing good and destroying all the works of the evil one. The Apostle Paul wrote a prayer for us,

> **I do not cease to give thanks for you, remembering you in my prayers, that the God of our Lord Jesus Christ, the Father of glory, may give you a spirit of wisdom and of revelation in the knowledge of him, having the eyes of your hearts enlightened, that you may know what is the hope to which he has called you, what are the riches of his glorious inheritance in the saints, and what is the immeasurable GREAT-NESS OF HIS POWER IN US WHO BE-LIEVE, according to the working of his great might...**
>
> **Ephesians 1:16-19**

Questions for Small Group Discussion

1. Are we living in a time when the church is holding a form of religion and denying the real POWER of God to heal and deliver?

2. Do we really need this kind of "power" experience today?

3. What are our options if we deny God's power?

4. How can we best represent this kind of power to the church?

5. What is the meaning of "Behold I give you power over all the power of the evil one?"

6. What is the difference between Exousia (Authority) and Dunamis (Power) in the Scriptures? Jesus gave us both. Luke 9:1

7. Are there signs of maturity for handling authority and power?

8. With the population of the world reaching seven billion in just a few years, will we need supernatural abilities to meet the needs?

CHAPTER SIX

"Prophetic Intercession"

Sixth Sign

God can make it absolutely clear when we are on target with His will or when we are out of line. One of the ways God does this is with the gift of prophecy. It is an extraordinary gift to help in the healing ministry, and is one dimension to the work of the Holy Spirit that is really opening up to the Body of Christ in our time. St. Paul said in I Corinthians 14: 1, **"Pursue love and strive for the spiritual gifts, and especially that you may prophesy."** We are not to just tolerate the nine spiritual charismatic gifts listed in 1 Corinthians 12: 8-10, but we are to earnestly desire and to seek after them, prophecy being number one. Why is prophecy so important? It is because it is a Spirit-charged utterance that speaks the Mind and Heart of God into his people, and that builds up, encourages, and comforts the people of God. The gift of prophecy is very effective in its operation.

This gift helps us stay in line with God's plan and purposes for our lives. When I went into the mainline church, I had non-denominational friends who were concerned that I might be limiting the Holy Spirit in my ministry. My bishop assured me God could move in the mainline churches, but my friends still worried that I would miss God for my life. One of my dear friends called me up and said he had a word for me. This was John Mark, who had been in the Glory Cloud with me, so my ears really perked up, especially my interior ear to the Lord. He said, "God told me to tell you dead wood burns the fastest." Well, I think I could figure that one out. My bishop had assigned me the task of interviewing with a very traditional Episcopal church. I really struggled with this: Should I take it; should I pass? I was a charismatic Christian, meaning I believed in the gifts of the Spirit operating in the church, and they had just had a war over whether or not to say the We Creed or the I Creed in the Prayer Book. The church was very conflicted. I thought I had better heed John Mark's prophecy, so I made a journal entry and decided to pray over it some more, for there had to be more to it.

A month or so later, I was asked to participate in a healing Eucharist in the old church in my home town where I used to play Rock and Roll in their parish hall. Some felt it might be good to redeem those old days, or atone for them in some fashion, so I accepted. We had a great time, and we even prayed for people to be healed at the end of the service. A lady then came up to me with a word of prophecy. I usually flinch when someone tells me they have a word, but I said, "Go ahead." She said, "You don't know me and I have never seen you in my life, and this is very strange and I do not understand it, but here it is: **Dead Wood Burns the Fastest**." I nearly fell down on the floor. I said, "Lady, you have no idea what you just did to me." Needless to say, I had just received the confirmation to taking the traditional church.

Hearing God in Prophecy and Dreams

The exciting part to prophecy is you learn that God can speak through so many different media, and each time one acts on it, the louder the voice becomes. God can speak through dreams, and prophetic words, and visions. Let me give you an example. It is about this very book you are reading. I started it over two years ago, but things were really dragging on. I had made little progress at all. At a conference in El Paso I went up for prayer and Bishop David Pytches prophesied over me that God was going to bless my writing on the computer. I looked at him in disbelief. How did he know? I never met the man in my life, and he knew my manuscript was safely filed away on the computer? "Way to go God," I said. So I labored on a little at a time. Later this last year I was wondering if I would ever truly write a book. It seemed I was so stuck.

Then, God gave me a dream that was as clear as a bell. In the dream I was leaning on a rail overlooking a body of water. I saw a man swimming in the water, and looked over to my left and saw a very large snake. I said, "Is that a snake I see?" At that moment the snake launched off for the man who was swimming. It grabbed him by the leg and was pulling him to what seemed like a sure death. I leaned over the rail and began to strike the snake with a newspaper. I beat the tar out of that snake until he let go of the man who then swam to safety.

Later I related this dream to a minister friend of mine whom I respect very much, Simon Purvis, from Lufkin, Texas. I asked what he thought, and this is what he said to me, "Jack that newspaper is the written word, some book, or some articles, or pamphlets, and you are going to destroy the works of the enemy with the written word." It was then that I told Simon about my book in the making, and we determined to pray through until the project was completed. I had "heard" God, and I now believe God is bringing this new ministry into fruition. Had I not written on after the prophecy, I doubt that the dream would have ever come. When one is faithful in a little, God helps to make us faithful in more.

One Prophecy Can Change
Your Whole Life

For the past 20 years, we have been looking for the authentic expression of God's love and power demonstrated through the organism the scripture describes as the River of God's blessing.

"Thou shalt swim in this river." So spoke the minister in this East Texas non-denominational church on the night of the Four Square minister's conference. I looked as out of place as a milk bucket under a bull. They all laughed when this Anglicized priest strode up to the prayer line after having been invited forward by the pastor for "a word." One lady said, " It looks like the right reverend has lost his dignity." However, when the young pastor began to pray over us and to speak out a word of prophecy, I sensed that something authentic was taking place.

I had always been told that whenever a person is speaking under the influence of the Spirit of God that there is a certain tenor and authority to the utterance. When this word went out over Anna Marie and me one could sense the presence and the power of the Holy Spirit. The presence of God was so incredibly rich. The Pastor brought us up to the front of the church and then he began to say,

For even now the seed that has been planted in thee shall begin to go over the walls, for men have tried to build walls and put thee into a category and say that say that he is like this, only to find that thou shalt escape out of their walls and their barriers, for thou shall begin to go over into places and over barriers that have been obstructed and held out against you before, but now know this, that thou are not going as a man or as one in a position, but thou art

going with the Holy Spirit even prompting and pressing thee. Thou shalt feel a time SO STRONGLY MOVED by the SPIRIT OF GOD that you cannot withstand it any longer until you go and speak with them. Thou shalt even go to speak to men in high places that have never been opened to you before. But son know that thou art not going as just a mouthpiece from a group of people but thou art going as an oracle of God and shall even speak as the promptings of the Holy Spirit. Thou shalt not go back the same way. For what the Lord has begun to grow in thee surely it will bring forth its fruit after its own kind. And thou shalt not be afraid of man. Thou shalt not even be afraid of what their considerations are. For what the Lord has brought thee into THOU SHALT be able to SWIM IN, THOU SHALT BE ABLE TO SWIM INTO THIS RIVER OF GOD AND IT SHALL LEAD THEE INTO PLACES WHERE THY OWN NATURAL ABILITIES WOULD NOT BE ABLE TO TAKE YOU. For son get ready and prepare thy-self. For the gift makes room for you, and it is even making room even to bring you before people of renown and name. For the brokeness shall come, and the brokenness shall create the humility of heart that is needed to be able to stand before these men. For the Lord has broken thee and these are times that you have thought in your mind, 'Lord am I where I need to be? Am I doing what I need to be doing?' And there have been many questions that have arisen up through thy family. And the Spirit of the Living God says to you tonight: Son, I have taken thee north so that you may go south, and it has appeared at times as a detour, it's appeared as a time that you have been lost and wandering around saying, 'Lord, have I missed you?' and the enemy has come and brought condemnation to you, making you feel like you've lost. FOR SON EVEN NOW THEE ART COMING OUT OF THE WILDERNESS, AND THOU ART COMING OUT IN THE POWER OF THE SPIRIT OF GOD. For thou shalt not eat the bread of stones. Thou shalt not even deliver stones any longer. FOR THE LORD SHALL CAUSE

THE BREAD TO BE IN THY MOUTH. OH TASTE AND SEE. THOU SHALT TASTE AND SERVE WHERE YOU ARE. IN YOUR OWN CHURCH IS ONLY A TEMPORARY PLACE WHERE THE LORD SHALL POUR INTO YOU, FOR HE HAS ANOTHER TABLE FOR YOU TO SERVE AT, AND IT WILL BE IN A PLACE THAT THOU COULD NOT GO BEFORE.

These words rang in my spirit. I clung to them as if they were hope itself. For all my life in the ministry, I have longed for the deeper things of God, even though I did not always know exactly what I was looking for, and in the weakness of my flesh never truly knew the cost nor wanted to pay the cost for moving deeper with God. But I did feel that there is so much more to God and his manifest presence than we had ever experienced. These words were recently fulfilled as Anna Marie and I left the world of the local parish to enter into the "broader table" of ministry to the whole body of Christ. I always thought that the "larger table" meant a bigger church with more to do. I had no idea it meant a healing ministry that would take us into Colorado, Kansas, Montana, Georgia, Canada, and even Great Britain. God does more than we can ask or think when we follow his will and his guidance. Prophecy is the # 1 gift to desire because it is the greatest asset to prayer. I guess so, when you consider how one prophecy can completely change your whole life when it is properly waited on, tested, and found to be genuinely of God. **Because of this gift, our lives will never ever be the same again.**

Praying Prophetically

When prayer becomes wedded to prophecy they become powerful weapons of our warfare. We do not have to struggle with the strongholds that are lodged in the church, our families, or our communities. We do not have to play guessing games—I think God will do this, or maybe God will do that. When God gets the message to us first as intercessors, he can get the message through us to others. It can be forth-telling of some event in a vision or a dream, and the beautiful thing is, it accomplishes God's interests. We can say, "I want God to heal the world, but what is God doing?" God may touch someone completely differently from the way I would. God is telling us what is on His mind. I believe we are coming into a greater level of effectiveness. I am freer today than I have ever been in my life. We are no longer telling God how to do it, and wondering why no one is getting healed.

We have seen powerful examples of this early on that are so fresh to our experience today. Our friends at the Church of the Redeemer, Houston, Texas, in the early 1970s saw God get involved in the action of prayer. They would spend hours in prayer in a little chapel in the basement of the sanctuary. Dr. Bob Eckhardt, who taught us how to "hear" God, would drive in from Galveston and pray at 5:30 A.M. along with about five elders in the church. A friend of mine told me that a young woman dreamed a dream that invoked a Spanish word. The dream would not let her go. She shared the word and the dream in the small prayer group. Nothing came of it, but the word would not let the young woman go, so she shared her burden again. Finally, someone decided to look the word up in the dictionary. It was the name of a small village in Mexico. They prayed and prayed over this until Dr. Bob felt led to get a small party together and to go down and visit the little town. They drove the distance until reaching the town, and pulled up to a stop sign, sitting there in their obvious American car. They sat there, wondering what in the world they were doing, when suddenly a man began to wave his arms wildly. He ran up to them yelling, "Are you the American doctor that Jesus said He was going to send us?" My! My! They ended up starting a clinic in that village that became a fantastic help to so many poor and sick people.

As I have said, Dr. Bob really knew how to listen to Jesus. He not only knew how to listen to Him, Dr. Bob knew how to obey.

One day while driving down the Southwest Freeway in Houston, he "heard" the Lord say, "Bob, pull over!" Bob immediately pulled over. A wreck occurred right where Bob would have been. He got out and ministered to the victims of this accident until all was taken care of, and then he went to sit in his car. Sitting there, with his head on the steering wheel, he asked, "God, why didn't you tell *them*?" God said right back, **"I did, Bob, but they weren't listening."** Bob learned to hear by obeying the Word. There is no other way.

Obeying equals Hearing

God is always speaking to us. Jesus said, **"Man does not live by bread alone, but by every word that is right now proceeding forth from heaven." Matthew 4:4** That is, the words from God's lips are right now issuing forth from heaven and showering us with wisdom, insight, revelation, and understanding, with guidance and directives necessary for our protection, preservation, healing, and deliverance from any works of darkness from the pit of hell. And all of this comes directly from time spent in the Scriptures.

Too often we know so little of the Bible even though we hear it read week after week in our churches. People simply do not know what it says. One can never know the voice of God without knowing the Scriptures intimately. Yet even those who study the Bible can still remain completely immature in the things of the Spirit. It takes doing it, and one hears, like Dr. Bob, by practicing the words. In **Hebrews 5:14** it says, **"But solid food is for the mature, for those who have their faculties trained by practice to distinguish good from evil."** The chief faculty of the spirit is "hearing", and to "disobey is to go deaf." Henry Drummond said obedience is to the spiritual body what the ear is to the physical body. When one obeys the Word, it gets easier the next time around, and hearing God becomes clearer. The voice becomes stronger and brighter. In the shallow waters of the River of Life it is absolutely essential to learn to obey and to hear, hear and obey.

"God is Spirit and those who worship him must worship him in Spirit and in truth."

John 4:24 We hear God with our spirit, but our bodies can literally become antennae for picking up the signals being transmitted from heaven. In this way, we are seeing the richness of Christ, and the fullness of His Spirit, come to the healing ministry. The Order of St. Luke the Physician (OSL) is a precious group of people devoted to bringing the healing ministry back to the Church of Jesus Christ. We are beginning to see the full complement of resources from heaven coming to bear in our work. As Jim Ross, our dear OSL friend, said recently, "I am no longer storming hell with my squirt gun."

We are waking up. We are realizing that when there is very little effect from healing ministry, it is time for prophetic intercession. There are many barriers to healing. Some of them are internal and some are external blocks. One time when I was preaching in a Pentecostal Church, I said the strangest thing. I said, "You remind me of Barney Fife on television. You have a gun and one bullet, but you can't find the bullet." I could not believe I said that, but they all agreed wholeheartedly. We called them forth for ministry and the whole front of the sanctuary filled up with people with two complete rows of people. We ministered healing and deliverance to people for two hours after that service. God brought the goods!

To Strike Once Only

Hearing God takes discipline. It is true that, **"... whoever does not receive the kingdom of God as a little child will never enter it."** **Luke 18:17** Alan Vincent, in teaching us about the Greek language, emphasized that it is a very precise language, with a rich variety of words. He explained to us that the word "child" in the above passage is *paedeon,* one of the words used to describe the father-son relationship. The word addresses the issue of discipline, guidance, and correction. Jesus referred to his disciples as *paedeon,* and, as you may recall he corrected them on many occasions. In Mark 2:17 Jesus refers to Peter, James, and John as the *Bo-anerges,* that is, the sons of thunder. They saw some others preaching in the name of Jesus, and they wanted to call lightning down from heaven upon them. Jesus rebuked them, and told them that they had a wrong spirit. When he disciplined them in front of everyone, he "struck them once," and that seemed to suffice. You never hear of the disciples calling down fire again from that point on. Therefore, when Jesus says that no one can enter the kingdom of God unless he become like a little child, he is not saying that one must be completely oblivious to the things of this world, gullible, and mindless. He is saying that the childish attitudes of selfishness, self-centeredness, and self-absorption will be corrected, redirected, and challenged if we heed his voice, and mind his ways with the responsiveness of a "once spoken to" child. Jesus was saying **that** kind of child enters the kingdom of God in its might and power. Jesus was saying if you can be corrected like a young child, "struck once only," you could enter the domain of the power of the kingdom. We are to learn in that place of hearing "once only" and obeying instantly. There is no quicker way to advance in the kingdom; there is no finer start.

Freedom from Carnality

We need the correction, guidance, and discipline of our Father, continuously. When we first enter the shallows of God's River, we are free to move about; our will is our own, and we do not fathom the thought that God's will can and will consume us for his good pleasure. Ankle-deep Christianity accommodates our independent spirit at first. It is fine and acceptable, in the trickle, to just taste a little of God without ever really getting wet. Many people have a great time in the shallows of the river. At first, the experience is wonderful. The water is cool and refreshing. We can reach down, grab a handful of water, splash about and play all day in the delightful beginning waters of God's love and joy. It is a little scary jumping into the unknown, but the River is inviting and harmless. Our impression of God at this level is often one of a sugar daddy. Church is all about my ills, my bills, and my thrills. We major in God giving to us one delight after another, keeping us entertained, and helping us to look good. Our sin, the one Isaiah talked about where each one has gone his or her own way, is never addressed. Our independence is rarely challenged. All we need to do is put on a cloak of religiosity and of good works, so we won't look so bad while we are all going our own way. We work harder to get God's approval, and tirelessly labor to win the approval of the people around us. We are told God is good, and will never require our lives for his (which always seemed to me to be a pretty fair trade). We are encouraged to splash around in all the promises and the blessings of God found in his Word.

Hearing God really should be the starting point for the ministry of the Holy Spirit in a Christian's life; this is where prayer is learned, and would to God we got this right from the very beginning in our training manuals for prayer. The gifts of the Holy Spirit would become a lot less mysterious and fearful. One can read all the books about the gifts of the Holy Spirit and get really charged up about it, but the learning is in the hearing and the doing. Hearing God is not difficult at all.

We are often asked, "How do you hear from God?" Well, ask this question: What does God say in his Word? If it is about disease, what does God's Word say?

> **Surely he has borne our grief and carried our sorrows.... But he was wounded for our transgressions, he was bruised for our iniquities; upon him was the chastisement that made us whole, and with his stripes we are healed.**
>
> **(Isaiah 53:4-5)**

He bore our sickness and disease on the cross. We can hear in it the voice of God put in prophetic phraseology, "**My child, I know your sickness, I know your disease, and I myself bore your disease on the cross; even now, I bear it away from you by my Spirit. I pour in my healing light and life, receive my life today. I loved you so much, I shed my precious blood to bring you to wholeness.**"

Can't you hear a loving God saying that to you? The shallow waters are the place to begin this process of hearing God, and doing what God says. Even a child can do this! In this very exciting place, God might speak to a person by showing them something in the spiritual realm. It just takes practice: dreams, visions, word pictures, flashes of words before one's spiritual eyes, these are all ways in which God communicates with us.

In the practice of "doing" the Word, one becomes fine tuned in hearing the voice of his or her Shepherd. For example, I was once in trouble as a pastor with a group of people in the church who really did not like my tactics on church growth. They were so offended at the way I did ministry that they were threatening to leave the church. Now, we are not in the business of running people off from the very institution that claims God's love for all people. So I went to this bishop and asked for help. He said these words, "Jack, if you will remain sweet, and return good for evil (I say evil here because to me the accusations and slander that went along with their unrest with me were disquieting.), you will come out on top." So, because these were scriptural words, and I knew they had merit coming from a bishop, I put the words into practice and went to every one of these unhappy people offering them an olive branch of peace. I even had a dream of a tornado coming to destroy a child lying naked on the ground. I fell across the child, but somehow knew with great peace, that it was going to be all right. The vortex of the tornado came right over the top of us, but did no harm whatsoever. I knew I had heard from God. The child represented the brand new work God had birthed in that church, and in truth all of the trouble in the church passed over. We did come out "on top." The church was spared any further disruption and discord, and was able to go on and actually quadrupled in size. Prophecy will line up in several ways that bring fruit to bear.

In our training sessions for healing prayer we teach that churches can become laboratories of safe love, and clinics for "hearing God." The gifts of the word of knowledge, the word of wisdom, and the discerning of spirits are fostered in this environment and greatly enhance the gifts of healings and miracles. Prophetic schools today are seeing the expansion of ministry gifts in this way. They practice hearing in secure environments where the gifts are cherished in an atmosphere of expectancy. If a "failure" occurs and someone misses God and gets it wrong, so what? There is no condemnation, and the person is free to get back up from the "miss" and get back into the game. Reminds me of the piano teacher who said, "Practice, practice, practice." If healing is "supernatural" then the door to that domain must be unsealed and accessible. Hearing God is the door.

Words of Knowledge Open the Heart to Faith

In John 4 Jesus is at a well with a Samaritan woman who is drawing water. She did not know Him. She did not have her eyes opened to see Jesus for who he was, until he spoke a word of knowledge and revealed her true condition. A word of knowledge or of wisdom is a supernatural bit of information that only God could know, but it is imparted to the believer for the purpose of letting the listener know that God is involved in the interaction and not just some human agency. This encounter with Jesus in the Bible reveals how utterly vital the other gifts of the Spirit are besides healing to the salvation experience in people's lives. The gifts break down the resistance and the hardness of heart that blinds us all. This woman was stuck in a pattern of repeated failure and chronic disappointment. Jesus revealed who he was by holding up to her a mirror of who she was,

> **"Go, call your husband and come back," Jesus said to her. "I have no husband," she replied. Jesus said to her, "You are right when you say you have no husband. The fact is, you have had five husbands, and the man you now have is not your husband. [Word of Knowledge] What you have said is quite true."**
>
> **John 4 16-18**

On occasion Anna Marie and I have spoken words of knowledge into situations and into people where there was oppression, unbelief so thick you could cut it with a knife, and re- sistance to the workings of the Holy Spirit. When the word is spoken in this supernatural way it brings faith forth. People open up to faith because they know they have heard from God for only they and God knew their condition. God has chosen in these instances to reveal a piece of hidden knowledge to get the people's attention that it is He that is speaking. This kind of prophetic intervention greatly enhances the healing event. Sometimes we will feel a pain in our own bodies that is not our own, and we know it is not ours. After speaking this out, and calling for that person to come forth for prayer, God heals them. We have seen it over and over again. At other times it is just a knowing and a speaking out of a condition almost before you are even conscious of what is being said. The speaking out of the word of knowledge or wisdom precedes the knowing of it. It is very economical too. I often say that Jesus was Jewish and very thrifty. One word of knowledge can pertain to several different people. Jesus never wastes anything, and He gets the most out of everything.

One time Anna Marie and I were in a youth worship conference. The only problem was: no one was worshipping. They were only observing a great little band. God had had enough I guess, and He gave Anna Marie the sensation in her chest of a serious panic attack. She knew it was not hers, so she stopped everything (I can't take her anywhere!) and called out this Word that God wanted to heal someone of panic disorder. She said, "Your heart races, you are gripped in fear, and you cannot sleep at night." No one moved. She did not flinch, but said, "We'll go to the back of the room and when you are ready you just come up to us for prayer and God will heal you." Well, a very attractive young lady came up and collapsed in Anna Marie's arms. She had been afraid to come forward, and she confessed that she was the one with the disorder. She was prayed for and healed. Then, another girl came up with the same condition. We prayed for her too. It was a two-for-one night with God opening the hearts of all those present. The next day the power of God fell on the whole conference. The worship was so strong, and so many were being ministered to by the Holy Spirit, that all the kitchen workers in the camp site came out to join us in worship. They said, "Somebody is havin' too good a time in here to miss."

This very day God is seeking worshippers who hunger and thirst for righteousness. God says they shall be satisfied. God is right now moving by his Spirit to take his church out of the bland drudgery of duty, and the restrictions of religious bondage, out into the waters of life that flow forth from the throne of God and his altar of forgiveness, refreshing, restoration, preservation, and provision like we have never seen before! These are people who experience worship as a dynamic encounter with the Living God who is able to do exceedingly abundantly above all we can ask or think. Prophecy and prayer are a one-two punch in the fight against evil. When we hear accurately what God is saying to the Church, and pray in line with his will, we become effective vessels.

A Criteria for Hearing Accurately

My friend Jackie White, a pastor from Church on the Rock in Lubbock, Texas has a five-fold criteria for testing prophecy:

1. Is it scriptural? Can you find a verse or verses in the Bible to back up what you are communicating by prophecy? Of course hearing things from God must be tested by the Scriptures, and by other witnesses, but it is an exhilarating enterprise.

2. Does it meet with biblical purposes? Does the prophetic word meet the criteria of building up the church, edifying the people, or comforting them? Does it bring the people of God in line with the purposes of God's kingdom in the earth to bring reconciliation and healing to a broken world? Does it free people?

3. Does the Spirit bear witness with the utterance according to **Romans 8:16, "It is that very Spirit bearing witness with our spirit that we are children**

> **of God, and if children, then heirs, heirs of God and joint heirs with Christ...."**

4. Does it bear fruit and give life to the listener? Or is it harsh, unloving, or perhaps rude? Does it come from love, or out of a spirit that is wounded or full of bitterness? What is the tone of the word, and what is its character? If it has an element of correction, is it delivered in the spirit of humility and grace?

5. And finally, does it bring peace to the people of God, or confusion? God is never the author of confusion.

Questions for Small Group Discussion

1. Can we "hear" God today? Does God still speak to us?

2. What role do the five senses play in hearing God?

3. Can a person be deceived by hearing "other voices?"

4. What is the proper protocol in the church for prophecy?

5. Can you see any advantage in joining prophecy to prayer?

6. What place do dreams and visions have in the church today?

7. How can you cultivate the ability to "hear" God? Is it a learnable experience?

8. Does obedience play a part in "hearing" God?

9. What are the guidelines for testing to see if a prophecy is truly from the Lord?

Chapter Seven

"How to Break Past Spiritual Barriers"

Seventh Sign

Indeed, we live as human beings, but we do not wage war according to human standards; for the weapons of our warfare are not merely human, but they have divine power to destroy strongholds.

2 Corinthians 10:3-4

I was at seminary. I had determined that I would fast without any food for eight days prior to giving my senior sermon. This was a sermon preached in the seminary chapel, and it counted a great deal towards graduation. I really wanted to preach well with good results. I did not feel comfortable with preaching the Gospel to these

Doctors and Philosophers. The environment was so intellectual and I did not want to preach an intellectual sermon. I had tried to do this before, as a Methodist minister, and all I did was put people to sleep. I wanted to see the Gospel make a real difference in the church again. I was desperate to see God work; yet, I felt so unworthy to bring this kind of message to such an elite group of professors and bishops.

I had a friend in the early days of seminary at Southern Methodist University in Dallas who was asked what he wanted to get out of seminary. He said he wanted to "really preach." The examining board said, "Yes, that's fine, we will help you to learn how to preach the Gospel text of the week." He said, "No, you don't understand, I want to REALLY preach."

That was exactly what I wanted for this sermon. I wanted to "really preach." I wanted it to count, so I entered a time of fasting and prayer. On the eighth day of the fast, I sat up in bed at 2:00 A.M. and began to sob. I began to REALLY sob. It was with groaning, travailing, and with loud cries so great that it was like what Paul spoke of in Romans the eighth chapter where the Holy Spirit will pray through us when we don't know how to pray as we should. I had to put a pillow over my head to muffle the sound.

Our dorm walls were paper thin, and I just knew I was going to wake everybody up thinking I was having appendicitis or a worse ailment. So, I buried my head in this pillow for about twenty to twenty-five minutes. Then, just as suddenly as it came, it was gone. You would think after a gut-wrenching encounter like that that I would have been exhausted, but I was at perfect peace, saturated in the presence of God, refreshed as though nothing laborious had occurred at all. Energized, I got up and began to write out my entire senior sermon. It was A to Zed. It was phenomenal! I was in total rest about it, and I knew something had broken in the "air" or in the heavenlies. It must have been that we were "waist deep" in the blessings of God, for extraordinary things were being birthed and were about to break forth.

The next day I broke my fast. I ate eight almonds (I heard they were good for mental enhancement, and I knew I was going to need all the help I could get addressing Doctors of Theology, Ph.D.'s, and professors, even bishops).

Several of us seminarians had been praying for Eleanor who had had a stroke, and was struggling with the failure of her kidneys. This was a very serious complication. This kidney condition related to the stroke and high blood pressure, and we knew we had to go to see her to pray for her. We were standing outside the library in a lively conversation when, suddenly, Eleanor came walking up the steps. She looked befuddled, puzzled, and even dazed. She said, "The doctors say I have been spontaneously healed." I said, "Eleanor you can't be here. We are coming to the hospital to pray for you." It was unbelievable. She was told to go home because the condition was completely resolved. An unseen hand slipped in on her in the night and touched her to relieve her from her suffering. One seminarian looked at us and said, "You don't mean God answered our prayers, do you?" How amazed she was that God actually healed someone like that!

The next day I was to preach. I called an old friend who knew how to intercede to see if she could dedicate the time at the exact moment I was to go into the pulpit. Chapel services were very predictable, so I knew the time to get her to pray. She did go into a prayer closet at that time thinking, I can give him ten minutes, for her schedule was so tight at her work place. She said God fell on her in prayer and she began to weep and cry. She prayed for 22 minutes. This was the exact duration of my sermon.

And did it work! God fell on that little seminary chapel. I want to tell you, the sermon was funny; it had ethos and pathos! There was electric energy in the atmosphere, and all I can tell you is: We had broken through!! A brother of mine in Christ came up to me and said, "You did it, and you pulled it off, you Charismatic." A professor, a good and decent man, came up to me and said, "I don't usually like sermons like that, but for some reason I liked yours. You're a Charismatic, aren't you?" The next day, the Pastoral Theology professor came in from an out of town assignment, and asked me, "What did you people do? This whole place is abuzz?" IT WAS GOD! God was all over that campus! That is all I can say. The power of the air had been broken, and the heavenlies were opened up to us.

Several days later my friend John told me of a dream his wife had. She saw the Angel of the Lord outside of the bishop's office located right there on the campus of the seminary. He had his sword drawn, and there were a host of demons hovering outside this window where the bishop's office is. They were like mitochondria in configuration. They were confused and hapless, flitting about. The Angel then raised the sword, they all came to attention in a strange configuration, and with one movement of the sword they were banished in thin air. Wow! What a dream. God showed me what it was. The Lord said the strong man rules until some- one stronger comes along and plunders his house (Matthew 12:29). The strong man who ruled over that area, on assignment from the kingdom of darkness, was keeping quite ac- tive. His house was plundered, rendered inef- fective. This explained the confusion and dis- orientation of their activities. In the dream the strong man was not present, only his "house." In a New Testament sense, his servants are considered his "house." They were vanquished foes in the heavenly battle won by the break through of the prayers and fasting of these "closet" Christians. I mean that as a great com- pliment, for Jesus told us that we should pray in secret, and your heavenly Father will reward us in the open.

The extraordinary thing about this was that a wonderful spirit-filled bishop arrived at that very site four months later to bring renewal and healing to the Austin area for the next several years. Travail and birthing prayer is a gift from God. It enables us to participate with God in bringing about a new order, a new and fresh movement of the Spirit. It causes the River to rise to the level of procreation, giving new birth to God's fallen and darkened creation. What a privilege to co-labor with God in His marvelous works. His River can flow into any and every situation. It is "**… beautiful for situations, the joy of the whole earth.**" **Psalm 48:2** His healing is unbounded by the banks and walls and constraints of human efforts to ignore and compromise His works.

Someone said that a stronghold is something that has a strong hold in some area of our lives. It could be personal or corporate, but it has to do with how people think, their patterns of thought, and how those thoughts trigger behavior, and hold us in bondage. The weapons of our warfare are very powerful for the "tearing down of strongholds." We can take those thoughts captive with the knowledge of Christ. The Gospel of Jesus is the power of God for salvation, and it carries a great ability to transform any situation. It is "beautiful for situations."

There is an experience of God that I am going to call Knee Deep Spirituality. The knees are the place in the body where we are exhorted to bow before God. By kneeling we demonstrate a posture of submission and of respect. We acknowledge the superior power and character of the one we bow to. It is an act of humility and of reverence. It has to do with the nature of our prayer walk with God and it has to do with the kind of intimacy in prayer that reflects our closeness to our Father God, who calls us to partner with Him in His Heavenly business affairs. This kind of spirituality brings us out of the shallow waters of "bless me, God" kinds of prayers into the intercessory life our Lord Jesus lived and prayed while He was here on this earth in a human body.

Breaker Prayer

It is absolutely appalling how church business kills fellowship with God. I had become a professional, a clerical robot working for God and not WITH HIM. This is what kills ministries and ministers. Most ministers pray less than fifteen minutes a day, and we wonder why there is so little power in our churches.

PRAYER BRINGS GOD ON THE SCENE! In **Luke 5:16** the scripture says, **"But he withdrew to the wilderness and prayed."** Several words later it explodes onto the page, **"...and the power of the Lord was with him to heal."** Prayer brings the presence of the Lord and his power?

I said count me in Lord. At one point in our ministry, my friends John Mark, Moses (a man from Nigeria who could pray wall paper off the wall), and Wanda Plummer (the woman who led me to the Lord in 1973), began to get together on Saturday mornings for nothing but prayer. Wanda was going to Bible School in Broken Arrow, Oklahoma, and she was full of nothing but FAITH! We were facing tremendous oppression and blockage in the spiritual realm. We were stuck. The four of us determined we would pray until heaven came down. And it happened, the power of God began to show up in manifestation. Many miracles and healings came forth in this little Methodist congregation. For example, a woman with terrible crippling arthritis in her hands and neck was prayed for at the back of the church with the door open to a 20-degree day outside the door. It got so hot praying for her I had to take off my jacket. She was totally healed—all pain left her body. She went home whipping that head around, showing zero pain in her hands and neck. I said YES LORD! This is CHURCH!!

One morning Wanda and I answered a distress call at a local hospital for a charity case. A little Mexican boy had been flown in with an aneurysm right behind his heart on his aorta. It was life threatening and everyone there was so torn up about it. The chances of recovery through the surgery to repair the artery were very slim. Wanda and I went up to the ICU glass room to pray and were quickly rebuked by a rather large nurse. But, we had been in prayer. Wanda saw another nurse named "Joy" who was about to go into that room, and she grabbed her. She said, "The anointing for healing is all over me for that little boy. If I lay my hands on you, will you go in there and put your hands on him in prayer? You see, the anointing on me will get on you, and you can pray for him (his name was Jaime) and God will heal him." Joy was a Christian so she said, "Okay, I'd love to." She went in that private room and laid hands on Jaime. Wanda and I left feeling quite confident that God had accomplished what He wanted.

The next day Wanda and I were just coming in the door to see how the surgery went, and they were rolling Jaime in a wheel chair. We said, "Hey, I thought you were going to have surgery?" The nurses, who were completely beside themselves, said, "Oh no, they took pictures of the aorta and there was nothing there. It completely disappeared." My, My, My! You talk about doing the "dance of joy." Prayer is absolutely amazing stuff! Why we don't spend all day in prayer is a mystery to me. God loves it, hell fears it more than anything else, and the world resists it with a vengeance! God called us out into the river to pray at knee level.

When we bend the knee we are saying to God, I want what you want. I yield myself to someone greater than myself, to that person's demands or desires. It indicates a willingness to obey the command of the greater party. I bent the knee on several occasions during this time of intense training in spiritual boot camp. Soldiers are not given the comfort of obeying only when they feel like it. Soldiers obey at any cost.

When we begin to pray with Jesus' heart for the Father the same results Jesus got in ministry will begin to become ours. Jesus said, **"The works that I do you shall do, and greater works than these shall you do." John 14:12** The river moves us to knee level. You sense a strong current in the movement of the river. God's life is becoming more pronounced in us. The river of God is beginning to displace our stance in this world. People see less of us and see more of God, and like John the Baptist we now know we must decrease so Jesus can increase. We are thirsting more and more for the things God is longing for. God is calling us out. Deep is calling to Deep!

Jesus ever lives to intercede now and we have His nature in us! **"As He is so are we in**

this world." (**1 John 2:13**) We carry within our bosom the heart of Jesus for praying to the Father. Jesus prayed in John 17 that the Father would give the disciples the same relationship that He had. That relationship cannot happen without prayer. In fact, it cannot happen without the kind of prayer life Jesus had.

Jesus prayed out loud at the tomb of Lazareth with loud groaning and travailing just like the kind Paul mentioned in Romans the eighth chapter where he said the Holy Spirit will intercede through a person who does not know how to pray in a given situation, and that the Holy Spirit would get the will of God as He prayed through the person. Romans 8:26 Jesus prayed aloud to let the people know how the Father always heard His prayers and to teach the people that He will always hear the prayers of any of His sons. John 11: 41-42 This kind of intimate prayer begets birthing prayer that begets a visitation from God into any circumstance. Then Jesus spoke the Word with great authority and the Lazareth miracle was birthed. It literally turned Jerusalem on its ears. Birthing prayer is mighty in its effects. It is the effectual fervent prayer of the righteous James talks about in his epistle in James 5: 18. He said this kind of prayer will avail much. James refers to

Elijah as a man similar to us with the same passions as we have, yet when he travailed in prayer a drought was birthed from heaven to serve to wake up the people of God and then at the right time, Elijah prayed again and it rained. I believe all of this effectual fervent prayer occurred in the birthing position as Elijah experienced birth pangs to bring forth the miracle of rain to break a prolonged drought.

The Apostle Paul in one of his epistles talks about a spirit of supplication and prayer. He wanted that spirit of prayer to come upon the people of God so they could prosper in the things of God and in the work of God. I believe a group of people, or even just two or three can come together and, in the spirit of prayer, beget a divine encounter of the kind that gives birth to new things in any situation. The prayer of travail is typical of a birthing kind of prayer. The Greek word is "odino." It means to give birth. It is where knee deep Christianity becomes waist deep. Ezekiel's waist deep river event is equivalent to a birthing of new Christian converts into the kingdom of God. It is also for the birthing of new and fresh encounters with God. In Isaiah it says, **"When Zion hath travailed, then she shall bring forth her children." Isaiah 66:8**

Going Deeper

Perhaps you are one who has been in church all of your life. Perhaps you have not come face to face with the Messiah who will "...offer you living water, the gift of God that will produce eternal life." You want the supernatural, you want the gifts of the Spirit, but feel stuck, and worship what you do not know. This is the beginning place. Oh you may have been in and out of church all your life, yet you know something is missing; your experience of God is lacking, and you know it. Ask him now to take away everything that separates you from a loving relationship with him. Ask Jesus to baptize you in the Holy Spirit. Confess all known sin and turn away from it. We will never see very much healing anointing in our lives, for ourselves, or for others at all, until we are DUNKED in the river of God's Spirit.

One time, when we were all praying in seminary, and we were making all these fabulous theological declarations about the ontological existential essence of God's ground of being, my wife piped up rather loudly and said, "God you're so smart!" It shut us all down with its profound simplicity. The truth is, He IS so smart. We have seen churches with forty-three people in Sunday attendance triple in size over night.

These churches would go on to grow five times over in the following years enjoying a significant move of the Spirit of God. All this happens because of "breaker" prayer. God knows how to give us help when we are without power, when we are directionless, and when we are stuck. He knows how to break us out of the barriers that are holding us back.

Biblical Intercessors

Think of some of the biblical intercessors that operated in the prophetic realm. They got a hold on God and would not let go. Think of Joseph, his dreams, and how he stood between God's people and a famine in Egypt. God raised him up in the worst of circumstances to come forth as a deliverer. I believe this is part of a very DEEP RIVER OF GOD in this hour of Church history. We are called to stand between God's people and the famine that is in the land for the Hearing of the Word of God. The church is languishing in many ways, dying in some ways, and in danger of total irrelevance to a generation of people. If we don't want to miss what God is doing in this time; we must connect up with the spirit of prophecy. As a friend of mine says, "Let's quit praying our laundry lists and find out what is on God's mind, what is on His heart, and pray through until the answer comes."

This has tremendous implications for the healing ministry in the church. There are times when we face heavy opposition to what God wants to do in our churches, our communities, or the institutions where we work. God wants to visit every place with His love, His grace, and His healing. When God comes to visit by His Holy Spirit, He brings all the gifts of the Spirit with Him. People's lives are altered permanently. Some are brought out of utter darkness into His glorious light. Many are healed and transformed from within, and miracles occur on a regular basis. All of this is done for the glory of the ONE who gave Himself so completely for us. For His sake, we are being sharpened and honed as instruments in His hand for the harvest that is so ready to be gathered into the storehouses. Breaker prayer is but one of the marvelous tools the Lord Jesus has given us to be effective prayer warriors for Him.

Glory Fires

Finally, one last story. Prayer will take a person into the glory realm where the fire of God resides. Not all rivers are placid, calming experiences. Beneath Ole Man River's waters lie the potential to level cities and towns. The torrential waters of adversity have the ability to level one's life as well, and it can come just as unexpectedly and quickly as a flash of lightning out of a blue sky. In June of 1983 I was flying high. We were fresh out of seminary and posted at our first three little churches. However, one of them did not stay little for long. After ten short months, the church had tripled in size. I would drive up on Sunday mornings and there would be cars lined up all up and down the highway on which the church stood. No room for parking. I remember walking into the sanctuary, and my wife would be able to tell the moment I walked in because the anointing was so strong on that place. It was like the wind would blow in the moment we all came together. Powerful things were happening in the spiritual realm. We were so hungry for God that we would have all night prayer meetings—singing, interceding, exhorting, and worshipping a Living God. One night my dear friend Simon Purvis was praying with us in one of these all-nighters, and a seventy year old man crawled up into his lap and began to speak in tongues as Jesus baptized him in the Holy Spirit. He was right there in Simon's lap! I was marveling at the sight of this Methodist so beautifully filled with God, when all of a sudden a hand grabbed me, pulling me into the parish hall, and said, "Get me out of here." I said, "Why, what's wrong?" He said, "I can't stand it in there!" I said, "Ok, ok, wait right here." So I went for Simon, because I figured, you know, "Jesus I know, Paul I know, and Simon I know, but who are you?" So when I got to him, I said to Simon, "Simon, come here! I need your help."

But Simon couldn't get the big man off of his lap. He was out in the spirit, and lay there like a beached whale. I then heard a banging noise, and rushed into the parish hall. The man was beating his head against our brand new wall, putting a great big greasy spot right there on that brand new wall. I got mad! I said, "Hey you, stop that!" I ran towards him when suddenly, he lunged at me like a raging bull. I grabbed him around the neck and down we went, taking the brand new coffee urn with us, breaking it and sending it in five directions. On the way down (I had heard somewhere that you were supposed to say, "Come out, come out"), I yelled, "Come out of him! Come out of him!" We hit the floor with a thud, and then it looked like he had broken his neck. I said to myself, "You killed him." But, when I looked at his belly it was quivering. By now Simon showed up, as well as about twenty others (I love this kind of meeting), and we stood the man up. I said, "Simon look at his belly; it's a void, it's a void. Just touch him on the forehead and he will speak in tongues." Sure enough, Simon did, and he did. He spoke in the most beautiful heavenly language.

The next day, his wife called. I said, "Oh my God, what did I do now?" She said, "What have you done to my husband?" I said, "Nothing, nothing, Simon did it!" She said, "No, you don't understand. He is like a pussy cat. What did y'all do?" Well, I told her the story, and to this day she marvels at her once angry, impatient, unbelieving husband who became like a lamb, full of love and peace, joy and happiness!

People just like you and me can get into real trouble. Did you know that guilt is a prison for the soul? There are many prisons people cannot escape today. Prison cells of worthlessness, shame, rejection, or fear... these are all impenetrable walls with no way of escape except the cleansing blood of Jesus Christ. He is the great emancipator:

The Spirit of the Lord God is upon me, because the Lord has anointed me; he has sent me to bring good news to the oppressed, to bind up the

broken-hearted, to proclaim liberty to the captives, and release to the prisoners; to proclaim the year of the Lord's favor, and the day of vengeance of our God; to comfort all who mourn in Zion—to give them a garland instead of ashes, the oil of gladness instead of mourning, the mantle of praise instead of a faint spirit. They will be called oaks of righteousness, the planting of The Lord, to display his glory.

Isaiah 61:1-3

Being in the river of God's healing has been the greatest experience of my life. It breaks people free from their bondage and brings them up out of the pit. I would not trade it for anything this world has to offer. If it were just for that one man who was delivered from a generational curse of anger and fear, I would go back and do it all over again for Jesus. The labor and intensity of breaker prayer is worth it all!

Questions for Small Group Discussion

1. How is your prayer life?
2. Do you see a connection between prayer and power?
3. Have you ever had an experience with "birthing prayer?"
4. What does it mean that God is looking for someone to "Stand in the Gap?"
5. Can we affect God with our prayers and change God's mind about situations and present circumstances?
6. What barriers or obstacles are you facing now that are preventing you from going farther in your walk with Jesus?
7. Would you be willing to partner with one other person to begin praying for spiritual breakthrough in your community?

CHAPTER EIGHT

"Miracle upon Miracle"

Eighth Sign

Does he who supplies the Spirit to you and works miracles among you do so by works of the law, or by hearing with faith?

Galatians 3: 5

Someone said that "busy-ness is not of the devil, busy-ness IS the devil." It was a typical workday for a priest in a seventy to eighty hour week. I had rushed to do a mercy funeral on the east side of Austin. The intercessors (very special people who prayed with me every morning at 6:00 A.M.) had sounded the yellow alert, that is, they had felt a deep urgency of the Spirit to call us to be cautious in our daily activities. Something down inside of them was uneasy. I heeded the message but I made very little change in my schedule.

The only time I have ever heard the audible voice of God was just before the time of these intercessory warnings. I was lying on my bed in my bedroom one late afternoon. I heard a voice behind me say, "Son, you're not waiting on me." I turned around startled that someone was in the room with me. There was no one there. I was very accustomed to the voice of God in Scripture, or in sermons, or even in songs of worship. I always thought that if He spoke to me it would be to tell me to build a bigger church, or to preach to the masses in China, or something like that. But this was an open rebuke. Only now do I know the full extent of what the Lord was trying to say to me.

I was in a terrible rush to get back to the office for the fifty things I had to do that day. After all, I was helping God build his church. Sitting at the red light my mind raced on, and when the light turned green, I pulled out in front of the bus next to me. The bus, however, did not move because he saw what was barreling down the road.

All I can say is, the Lord is good. I do not remember the impact of the twenty-ton asphalt truck hitting my little Geo Metro. Being that this compact car was mostly aluminum, it looked like a crushed soda can after being smashed and pushed one hundred plus feet down the feeder. My life was suddenly halted, and would hang in the balance on a thin thread for the next twenty-four hours.

The policeman who drove up on the scene said, "That person did not make it." I lay there behind the shattered windshield being attended to by a doctor who just "happened" to be there. She was applying pressure to a severe cut over my right eye. I gasped for air and saw the young man who ran the red light pacing in a panic in front of the car. All I could mutter was, "Jesus, help us."

We just "happened" to be a couple of blocks from one of the best trauma centers in the country, and when I arrived they carefully relayed me to a stretcher in the emergency room. My wife, Anna Marie, came rushing in and asked me what happened. I cried, "Honey, I ran a green light." She just sighed and held my hand. My back was killing me, and my thinking was that it was broken, but after taking x-rays, the trauma team called in a cardio-vascular surgeon.

The aorta is a large artery that comes out of the top of the heart and loops around to branch off in two directions, upper extremities and lower extremities.

It had ruptured upon impact in the collision, and as I put it, "Blew out like a tire." I had lost many pints of blood and was slowly losing the feeling in my legs. The surgeon came into the room where I was and poked me with a needle in my foot.

He asked, "Did you feel that?" I said, "No sir, I did not." He said, "Mr. Sheffield, you have lost a lot of blood to the trunk nerve that goes to your legs, and I am afraid you are never going to walk again." Immediately, I saw in my mind's eye Anna Marie pushing me in a wheel chair, but this is what came out of my mouth, "Doctor, somebody up there likes me, and besides you are going to do a great job." I looked at Anna Marie and blacked out from the pain.

What is in You Comes Out in a Crisis

I have often marveled at that response. The normal reaction to terrifying news like that is to plow into despair and fear, but what came out of my mouth was FAITH. Wonder where that came from? For almost twenty years I had put in the Word, the Word, the Word of God. I studied it, lived it, ate it, breathed it. When I needed it the most, the Scriptures were there for me. I have always believed that in a crisis, what is in you is going to come out, and to this day I thank

God that what was in me gave birth to miracle upon miracle.

The staff rushed me into surgery and patched me up. Besides the ruptured aorta, they found a torn and severely macerated (smashed) liver. They found eight broken ribs with compound fractures, and a hip broken in two places. A Dacron graft was placed around the aorta to seal off the loss of blood. After the surgery they said that if I lived for twenty-four hours, I might make it.

During this operating room drama, the emergency room looked like a convention of ministers. There was so much prayer going on, especially in the chapel. During this time, the most amazing thing happened. While calling for prayer support on the telephone, Anna Marie was approached by the young man who ran into my car. He almost fainted from the emotion of the moment, and nearly collapsed in the arms of a priest standing with my wife. He asked forgiveness and Anna Marie graciously embraced this crying boy to assure him it was going to be all right. They prayed with him to receive Jesus as his salvation, his security, and his Lord. From what they tell me, there were very few dry eyes in the waiting room that evening. Someone would say to me later, "Man you'll do anything to see them come into the Kingdom." Not the best way to grow the church, but God will take every situation and turn it into good when He is in the lead and at the head of our lives. Another miracle took place as I was in a very critical time of my recovery.

My blood pressure suddenly went off the charts. It reached three hundred over two hundred (that is 300 over 200), and the nurses called for the doctors to intervene. They said they were losing me. Amazingly, there were several people in the chapel praying for me. Fortunately for me, these prayer people were highly skilled in all kinds of prayer, and not just the kind of prayers of pleading or begging God to do something. These people were what we call "prayer warriors" who knew that there are times where you do not ask God for anything, you take command of the situation with what is called The Prayer of Command, or The Prayer of Authority. The scripture says that when we do not know how to pray, the

> **... Spirit helps us in our weakness; for we do not know how to pray as we ought, but that very Spirit intercedes with sighs too deep for words. And God, who searches the heart, knows what is the mind of the Spirit, because**

the Spirit intercedes for the saints according to the will of God.

Romans 8:26-27

In other words, the Spirit knows how to pray THROUGH the prayer warrior to get the will of God.

A woman named Carol was praying in the chapel, and she had no idea what I was going through in the ICU room. She "saw" by the Holy Spirit in a vision that death was coming to get me, and she rose up in the Spirit of God and rebuked the spirit of death. She did not ask or beg, she commanded! When my wife compared notes with her later, they discovered that at the same time she had that prayer experience, my blood pressure began to drop to life preserving levels until I was out of danger. I also thank God for the Order of St. Luke the Physician because they train people to pray with all manner of prayer to get results like that. I owe them my life. Every church needs an Order of St. Luke chapter for these reasons. Someone sometime is going to need powerful prayer intervention to make it out of his or her crisis.

I had an experience during that urgent time that is hard for me to articulate. I, like Paul the Apostle, do not know if I was in the body or out of the body. I cannot tell you if it was an open vision or an actual out of the body experience or a dreamlike state. All I know is I was lying in Jesus' arms, and I believe He was being influenced by the prayers that were taking place. I sensed, or just knew without words, that He was giving me a choice to stay or return to my earthly body. I thought/spoke, or said by thought without words that, "Anna Marie could not take another one." We lost a precious little boy in 1986 to Leukemia. His name was Stephen Thomas, and I just knew Anna Marie could not bear another loss, so I asked, "Can I be a part of the harvest?" Jesus said, "If you want to." The next thing I knew, I was in my body telling my friends at bedside that He had blue eyes. The best way to describe them was the look of "many waters."

After stabilizing for several days, I was discharged from ICU and moved to a regular room. There were so many problems to tend to, especially the liver function. My numbers were off the chart. What they did to treat the liver in surgery was to piece it together as best they could and pack it with a kind of foam. It was so damaged that there was talk of a possible transplant, and I was to be in the hospital for at least six weeks. The pain of eight broken ribs made it difficult to even breathe.

At one point I was in a very serious crisis, and Bishop Cox called. He said, "Jack, Betty and I have been in prayer and the Lord tells us you are going to be one-hundred percent, but you are going to have to walk through some things." I whispered, "Thank you, Bishop," and passed out.

I could barely speak, my voice was so weak. It so happened that during the surgery on the aorta the doctor had to push back a nerve that wraps around the aorta and is linked directly to the vocal chords. Can you believe that? The Bible is so amazing! **"Out of the abundance of the heart the mouth speaks." Matthew 12:34** My first sermon when I reported back for duty at the church was "The Mouth Bone is connected to the Heart Bone."

The greatest miracle I have ever personally experienced occurred on the seventh day of this ordeal. To the amazement of my doctors, all of my liver functions gave normal readings. The chief surgeon came by on several occasions with his staff and called me the "miracle man."

On the ninth day they took the drainage pipes out of my back, and stood me up at the bedside. (The hardest thing I have ever done physically in my life) The next day they walked me on crutches to the bathroom, then to the door.

On the eleventh day they walked me to the nurse's station, and then sent me home. Within several weeks I made my first appearance at church on crutches, and I preached within several weeks of that. My recovery was phenomenal to say the least.

The Seed Within

I could see that the one-hundred percent recovery was in sight, but I was having a very difficult time with my voice. The nerve damaged in the surgery was threatening my career as a professional speaker. In fact, the doctor assigned to help me with the problem told me I would need a plastic strip placed over the "bowed" vocal chords to keep me from losing my voice forever. This just did not set well with me. I heard the words of Bishop Cox down inside me whenever I would pray about it: "one hundred percent". At times the circumstances were yelling at me, "You'll never be the same. You won't ever speak well again." I even grew polyps on one chord because I would not stop talking or singing. But that little seed down inside of me would not let up; it knew that bishop had heard from God. It was not a loud voice at all, but it kept saying, "One-hundred percent— one-hundred percent."

How many people are in that place today? Their environment or their situation is crying out, saying, "Failure! You'll never make it! It's impossible." There are always those voices that cry out, "It's for everyone else, but not for you!" But if we just hear from God and His Word, even though it may just be a little seed down inside of us, it has the power to grow up and overcome all the voices that come out of the shadows of this world.

I persevered for months in therapy and treatments when one day a great Eye, Ear, Nose and Throat man named Dr. Richard Stassney, looked down my throat to find that all the polyps had disappeared and the vocal chords had gone back to their original position. I danced and shouted as I realized I was now one hundred percent well. Of course, my wife tells me I am one hundred percent except for brain damage, but I remind her that I had brain damage before the wreck.

We are for Signs and Wonders

Miracles do happen today. I am one; in fact, I am a sign and a wonder. **Isaiah 8:17** says, **"We are for Signs and Wonders."** Let me borrow, if I may, from John's final words in his gospel:

This is the disciple who is testifying to these things and has written them.... But there are also many other things that Jesus did; if every one of them were written down, I suppose that the world itself could not contain the books that would be written.

John 21:24-25

John said these things were written down so that the reader may KNOW that Jesus is the Christ, and that by believing in Him a person might have eternal life, or *Zoe.* That eternal life today includes healing, deliverance, protection, and extraordinary provision—the full spectrum of salvation. My testimony is the same as John's for, **"Jesus Christ is the same yesterday, to-day, and forever." Hebrews 13:8**

The eight signs in this book are a testimony to that fact, and that the knowledge of the Lord is ever increasing and reaching flood stage. There are so many more I could tell about, but there really is not enough room. These signs are indicators to me and I hope to others that there is today an out-pouring of the Holy Spirit in the Church to rival that of the first and second centuries. People are coming into the Kingdom of God en masse. It is estimated that nearly seventy million people worldwide came into the Kingdom last year, twenty-five million in China alone. The total number of born again, spirit led Christians now approximates the seven hundred million mark across every nation on the planet. It says in **Isaiah 11:9,** "**...for the earth will be full of the knowledge of the Lord as the waters cover the sea.**"

Questions for Small Group Discussion

1. What is the difference between a miracle and a healing?

2. Are you uncomfortable talking about miracles?

3. Have you ever experienced a miracle?

4. Do we still live in a Newtonian Universe where everything is predictable and calculable? Or do we live in an Einsteinian Universe where things are unpredictable and full of surprises?

5. What part do signs and wonders play in convincing people of their need for a relationship with the Living God?

6. Are you prepared to participate in the greatest harvest of souls the world has ever seen?

CHAPTER NINE

A Two Thousand Year Flood Plain

Again he measured one thousand, and it was a river that I could not cross, for the water had risen; it was deep enough to swim in, a river that could not be crossed.

Ezekiel 47:5

When a river breaks out of its banks and enters the flood plain it is completely indiscriminant. It does not care whether it washes over brick houses or wood frame, over Caucasian houses or Hispanic, over Episcopal barns, or Baptist, over French fields, or English. Rich, poor, down, out, it does not matter. It does not care whether a person is a Democrat or a Republican, speaks Swahili or Polish. The river goes anywhere it wants to. It will wash away any obstacle in its path. There is no resisting it when the power of that river is forceful enough. In our time God is going to send a RIVER of LIFE that no barriers will be able to contain, no dams can hold, and no reservoirs restrict. All the power of heaven will be behind this RIVER, all the might and strength of the RAINS of HEAVEN will feed this torrent, and this RIVER will make a certain and definite path. It is for healing the nations.

We are, as God's possession, a "people of the river." **The Body of Christ is about to go SWIMMING.** To SWIM in God's Healing River is to fulfill our prophetic destiny and to honor our heritage as Christians in these last days of human history as we know it. Transformation is in the air. **1 Thessalonians 1:10** says Christ is coming **"...to be glorified in His saints on that day, and to be marveled at by all who have believed."** Christ's Bride is about to come out of the closet. Jesus is to be "glorified" in her. This means that the tangible glory cloud of God is going to be recognizable upon the people of God.

The later stages of God's Healing River in Ezekiel forty-seven point to an "over-the-head" experience of the ministry of the Holy Spirit. Metaphorically, it speaks to a total Spirit-filled condition in the Church. Paul says the Church is God's body, **"...the fullness of him who fills all in all."** **Ephesians 1:23** Again he says,

In him the whole structure is joined together and grows in to a holy temple in the Lord; in whom you also are built together spiritually into a dwelling place for God.

Ephesians 2: 21

The meaning of these texts refers to the advanced stages of growth and maturation of those whose faculties have been trained by experience, and who have weathered the fires of trial and adversity by entering into the Lamb's war on sickness and disease of spirit, soul, and body. The "overflow" experience is about the full ministries, operations, administrations, and demonstrations of the Spirit of the Living God who is moving mightily in the Church. This is what is meant when we say "swimming" in God's Healing River.

The Dancing Hand of God

There are signs that we are moving into this advanced stage, the "fullness" of God in church. For example, in a recent healing mission at St. John the Divine Episcopal in Houston, Texas, there were over twenty words of knowledge given BY THE PEOPLE. God was healing people all over the room. This has been called the "dancing hand of God." The word for manifestation comes from two Latin words: *manos* (hand) and *festus* (gala, or at the root meaning, dancing). This is where the body of Christ plunges into the river of God's gifts, and spiritual blessings saturate the room of meeting. One can hear the Lord saying, "Come into who you are in Christ, come to know what your inheritance is. It is rich beyond imagination. Be filled with the Holy Spirit, and receive power to become a witness in this time. There is nothing more exciting anywhere in the universe. Take the plunge and dive into what the Lord God Almighty is doing in the earth today. It will affect you for all eternity."

Another example of the "dancing hand" and swimming in the river is when I was giving a workshop in the 2001 North American Order of St. Luke Conference in Longview, Texas. It was a fabulous time together with so many great speakers like Francis MacNutt, Bishop William J. Cox, Mike Flynn, and others. The Spirit of God was very present, and when it came time for the workshops we were pumped! We were wall-to-wall with people jammed into a little classroom. When it got started the most extraordinary thing happened. The Holy Spirit fell on all of us. The workshop was supposed to be for one hour, but after three hours the smoke cleared and we stumbled out of the room with people still ministering to each other. Every one of the nine charisms in I Corinthians 12 operated in that three-hour time span. There were healings, miracles, prophecy, tongues and interpretation, faith, word of knowledge, word of wisdom, and discerning of spirits. There were several people who went through deliverance, and a spontaneous, unrehearsed spirit song was birthed right there out of the Spirit of God. It was DEEP RIVER, and it was a prophetic sign of what the Lord God is leading his people into. We did not see the golden light, but He was there! God was manifesting all over the whole body. As the psalmist said,

> **How very good and pleasant it is when kindred live together in unity! It is like the precious oil on the head, running down upon the beard of Aaron, running down over the collar of his robes.**
>
> **Psalm 133:1-2**

The psalmist was using the person of Aaron to stand for the modern priesthood of the believers. That's all of us who believe in God. And those of us who were there that day in Longview could have said the Lord was so marvelously generous in the outpouring of the oil of His Holy Spirit that is was running, not only down into our collars, but down to our toes!

Our work called Deep River Ministries was birthed out of that workshop. The tape of that session went out everywhere, and before we knew it Anna Marie and I were being asked to speak all over the country and beyond. Ever since that conference our desire is to see Jesus bring His healing love and power to a generation of hurting and suffering humanity, and to see him inundate a generation with a floodtide of mercy.

The Current Condition

There are signs all over the Church that the waters are rising. There is considerable interest in the Holy Spirit in general in the church. The perception I used to have of the present day "body" was a big mouth (wonder who that could be) and anywhere from 80 to 300 ears. What kind of body is that? That is not a body. This was scandalous compared to what The Lord Jesus has promised us in the fullness in His Word! The people of God are being cheated out of the riches of glory that are in Christ Jesus. What is worse is that the people of the world are being denied access to the treasures of God's grace towards them. God has had trouble getting his program past his own people! All that is changing with the acceptance of the "priesthood of all believers." Now practically every member of the church can have a ministry. It means we are seeing a wider field of participation, and a greater dimension of spiritual life and power. The job of advancing healing in the kingdom is so great it is going to take every one of us to "get into the flow." It is just like Peter said in Acts, Chapter 2,

In the last days it will be, God declares, that I will pour out my Spirit upon all flesh, and your sons and your daughters shall prophesy And your young men shall see visions, and your old men shall dream dreams. Even upon my slaves, both men and women, in those days I will pour out my Spirit, and they shall prophesy. And I will show portents in the Heaven above and signs on the earth below....

Acts 2:17-19a

Prophecy Schools and Healing Schools have been raised up to assist the Church in advancing these ministries. They both teach the sensitivity and responsiveness to the ministry of the Holy Spirit, and have seen the two streams of this River coming together in a big way in our time. Not long ago, I heard a nine-year-old girl get up in front of hundreds of worshipping Christians and speak out a prophecy that had tremendous depth and meaning.

The Holy Spirit of God is gifting all of the Church with the power of Gospel of Jesus Christ. This power is increasing in the present time, and will culminate in the greatest marriage of evangelism and healing the world has ever seen. The cry of affliction is once again rising to heaven, as in the days of Moses, and God is hearing the plea of the nations. Is there a God in heaven who cares? The healing ministry given to the church is the direct answer to that prayer. We must answer the call.

Charismatic gifts of the Spirit are of great interest to the people in the pew who are attracted to the power of the Spirit. In our society, there are many un-churched people who are being drawn to the supernatural, as well. People today are more aware of the limitations in confronting human dilemmas with human resources alone. Folks "out there" are able to intuit the need for a source of help beyond the confines of human ability. They are searching for answers, for some kind of benevolent intrusion into the problems they face. They are open to being surprised by miraculous events. However, this hunger poses a real problem. If the curious are not directed to reliable, Scriptural based resources that deal with spiritual phenomena, they may turn to more unreliable, dubious sources with materials that do more harm than good. The Church must meet this need for sound teaching.

Impact on Leadership

A great desire on so many hearts today is coming to pass. Pastors are being drawn into a healthy, trusting, and cooperative relationships with laypersons to bring the finest quality of prayer and healing ministry to the church. This is expanding the pastoral base to care for more people, and save pastors from burnout. They are experiencing a joy and an excitement that is unparalleled in church history, and are pointing the way for others to follow. Ministers today are dealing with the tough inner issues of pride, fear, control, and discouragement. God is the great encourager, and he is about fostering and nurturing the maturation process of the Body of Christ. In Ephesians Paul writes of this:

And his gifts were that some should be apostles, some prophets, some evangelists, some pastors and teachers, to equip the saints for the work of ministry, for building up the body of Christ until we all attain to the unity of the faith and of the knowledge of the Son of God, to mature manhood, to the measure of the stature of the fullness of Christ; so that we may no longer be children, tossed to and fro and carried about with every wind of doctrine, by the cunning of men, by their craftiness in deceitful wiles.

Ephesians 4:11-15

This is where history has been pointing for the millennia, where the Spirit is taking us: healing leaves for all the peoples of the earth (Rev. 22:2). However, to get there, one must realize that this RIVER, like most, insists on its own unpredictable current and direction, unless one only stays in the shallow waters of the river. The real danger for the church in our time is that she will stay in the superficial waters of apathy and indifference, and let a dying world decay in its agony. Another potential snare for the church is that it will continue to relegate "giftings" to the precious few, the professionals, and the elite class of those who "have it." God wants the anointing oil of "giftings" from the Holy Spirit to flow over the whole of God's people: the unity of expressions, manifestations, and demonstrations of what God can do in any meeting or setting where the church is in worship. Gifts, demonstrations, and expressions of the Holy Spirit start at the top and flow down the head, down the shoulders all the way down to the bottom of his feet. This means EVERY person is anointed by the Holy Spirit and becomes a potential minister in any given setting. This is what real unity is in the Body of Christ. It is a divine mandate to loose the flow of the Holy Spirit over the whole of God's people.

We all have the same opportunity to be anointed by the Lord to operate in our respective giftings, free from religious fear, restraint and restriction. Risky business, but so very blessed. The real hope for the world is that the Church will awaken, as the sleeping giant she is, and begin to put on her strength and her beauty; that the church will come alive with all the power, authority, and giftedness God intended for her to wear.

Finally, Anna Marie and I travel all over the country doing "healing missions" and conferences for churches and "para-church" organizations, and what we find is this:

1. There are so many people in our churches who are hurting and in pain. Many churches are still uninformed about the gifts of the Holy Spirit that destroy disease, depression, inner bondages like unforgiveness and bitterness, emotional instability, and plain old discouragement. Many churches still fear the healing ministry. How can the church heal the nations when it is so sick itself? In our world there is a great hunger in people for knowledge and understanding with regard to health and wholeness as it pertains to the spiritual aspects of healing. The "disease" people are experiencing is more than physical; it is emotional and spiritual; it is individual, familial, and societal.

2. "In the know" pastors are seeking ways of expanding the pastoral base of their congregations so that more people in duress receive greater care. For example, church leaders are entrusting more responsibility to "lay chaplains" for pastoral care. These leaders are concerned about excellence in the quality of care. Healing is directly tied to

pastoral care in this new paradigm for church ministry. Lay chaplains need training and encouragement. There is a need for quality teaching materials.

3. The new paradigm for ministry includes the implementation of team concepts. There is a tremendous need to teach and train healing "teams" within churches, and to find new materials to illumine, inspire, and display the demonstration of a healing ministry in very practical terms.

It is time for the "people of the river" to come forth. **It is time for the Body of Christ to go swimming!**

Soundings Taken from the River

This manuscript speaks to the history of healing ministry that has taken place in past eras of the church, and how The Holy Spirit has moved into the human predicament answering the plea of a dying and crying humanity. The following is a glimpse into the progression and movement of just a few significant healing ministries. This river has emerged from its subterranean depths with great power off and on for 2,000 years now.

God's Healing River is evident throughout the Scriptures. This river from God ebbs and flows in the history depicted by the people of Israel and most notably is displayed by Moses who held up a Bronze Serpent and God healed all the people bitten by snakes in the wilderness. Numbers: 21: 8-9 Throughout the wilderness experience this river followed the wandering people of God. There were distinct moments of visitation from God that provided healing and restoration for the weary travelers. Moses smote the rock and water poured forth giving life to the people (Numbers 20:11). The Psalms are replete with accounts of healing from the hand of God, especially Psalm 22 in the foretelling of the cross of Christ. Isaiah prophesied of waters flowing in the desert to give drink to a dry and thirsty land (Isaiah 35:7).

The book of Acts is filled with accounts of healings and miracles, some of which caused such a stir that wholes cities came to the saving knowledge of God in Christ Jesus. But many do not know much about how healing and miracles continued on beyond the original apostolic ministries. Origen, who lived c.185 AD— c.254 AD, is believed by some to be the greatest scholar of the ancient church. He clearly acknowledges the power of the Spirit to gift God's people with miracles and healings.

> I think the wonders wrought by Jesus are a proof of the Holy Spirit's having then appeared in the form of a dove, although Celsus, from a desire to cast discredit upon them, alleges that He performed only what He had learned among the

Egyptians... And there are still preserved among the Christians traces of that Holy Spirit which appeared in the form of a dove. They expel evil spirits and perform many cures and foresee certain events according to the will of the Logos. And although Celsus... may treat with mockery what I am going to say, I shall say it nevertheless: that many have been converted to Christianity as if against their will, some sort of spirit having suddenly transformed their minds from a hatred of the doctrine to a readiness to die in its defense, and having appeared to them either in a waking vision or a dream of the night. Many such instances have we known, which, if we were to commit to writing, although they were seen and witnessed by ourselves we should afford great occasion for ridicule to unbelievers, who would imagine that we... (had) invented such things. But God is witness of our conscientious desire, not by false statements, but by testimonies of different kinds, to establish the divinity of the doctrine of Jesus.[1]

However, as quickly as it came, it ebbed away into the shadowy recesses of the Dark Ages, not to be seen again for centuries to come, except in pockets of God's blessings. The river went underground and became a subterranean stream only to surface occasionally to give precious drink to chosen generations. From that moment on in history, the river has emerged at certain times to bring refreshing, healing waters to the desolate, dry, and desert land.

One place where the river emerged in full splendor was in the life of Augustine of Hippo in the 5th century. Augustine began to experience the miraculous healing power of God in his ministry, even though he had renounced healing as bogus early on in his priesthood. He said in his book, *City of God,*

> ... once I realized how many miracles were occurring in our own day and which were so like the miracles of old and also how wrong it would be to allow the memory of these marvels of divine power to perish from among our people. It is only two years ago that the keeping of records was begun here in Hippo, and already, at this writing, we have nearly seventy attested miracles.[2]

Augustine of Hippo, after years of denying the power of the Spirit to heal, succumbed to its wonderful effects. In his *Homilies on I John,* Augustine states,

> Those miracles are all recorded, as we know, in the Scriptures, which never lie.... And in fact, even now miracles are being performed in Christ's name either by his sacrament or by the prayers of the memorials of his saints, but they do not enjoy the blaze of publicity which would spread their fame with a glory to equal that of those earlier marvels.... A Miracle that happened in Milan while I was there, when a blind man had his sight restored, succeeded in becoming more widely known because Milan is an important city, and because the emperor was there at the time. A great crowd had gathered to see the bodies of the martyrs Protasius and Gervasius, and the miracle took place before all those witnesses.... It was there that the darkness, in which the blind man had lived so long, was dispelled; and he saw the light of day.[3]

Again Augustine said,

> There was one miracle performed in our city... so widely famed that I should imagine no one from Hippo failed to witness it

or at least to hear about it. (He tells of the healing of a young man with sever palsy at the shrine of St. Stephen.) He had been cured, and he was standing there, completely recovered, meeting the stares of the congregation. Who could then refrain from giving praise to God? The whole church was filled in every corner with shouts of thanksgiving... the church was packed and it rang with the shouts of joy: 'Thanks Be to God! God be praised.' The cries came from all sides; not a mouth was silent... They rejoiced in the praises of God with wordless cries, with such a noise that my ears could scarcely endure it.[4]

These miraculous healings had great effect on Augustine, so much so, that he was the first person to formulate the criterion for determining whether an alleged miracle is truly from God or not. That formula is still being used today. All this must certainly have been a rich blessing in the dark age of corruption, barbarism and brutality. God's River was following the people through the dark, desolate places into the Medieval Age.

Shortly after Augustine, Cuthbert began to experience the River of God's Healing in what is now the British Isles.

The life Cuthbert led at Lindisfarne is summed up in a few words by the monk of Lindisfarne: 'He lived there according to the Holy Scriptures, uniting together the contemplative and the active life; and gave us a rule of life which he drew up, and which we now observe, together with the rule of St Benedict.' ... Moreover, by his miracles, he became more and more celebrated, and, by the earnestness of his prayers, restored to their former health many that were afflicted with various infirmities and sufferings; some that were troubled by unclean spirits, he not only cured whilst present, by touching them, praying over them, or even by commanding or exorcising the devils to go out of them, but even when absent he restored them by his prayers, or by foretelling that they should be restored; amongst whom also was the wife of the Praefect....[5]

The Franciscan movement, birthed by Francis of Assisi, spread the gospel all over the world in the 1200s. It is reported that Francis saw many miracles. The Reformation saw Martin Luther transforming the landscape of religious Europe, and the mighty Great Awakening with the Wesley brothers who saw Great Britain revived and spared from the same destructive doom that visited France in that an era of violence and social anarchy. The Wesleyan Revival was attended to with signs and wonders from the supernatural realm.

A more recent example of the river surfaced in Rome, New York in the 1800s where the famous evangelist Charles Finney and Father Nash went in and prayed down an out flowing of God's favor and might in torrential waters. Father Nash was a powerful intercessor for Finney. This town, like so many of that day, was caught up in worldly pleasure and vice. People's hearts were cold and far from the love of God. But as Nash prayed, a strange power began to lurk about in the streets, in the homes, and in the businesses of this municipality. Several weeks later, the preacher Finney was invited into a judges' house for a private meeting with substantial town leaders. The living room was full of influential and prominent people—the attorneys, doctors, and the elite businessmen of the city. The conviction of God was so strong as he shared the Gospel that he could barely speak above a whisper. He knew that if he spoke up at all the very sound of his voice would shatter their souls into thousands of little pieces for God was so strong on them! I would love to go back and do a "dig" into how this River of Conviction and Repentance witnessed the transformation of that little city in New York. What remnants and artifacts of godliness, and virtue would an excavator find? What blessedness would be unveiled? What heritage revealed? I'm sure this city that camped by the river of God found healing in the leaves of its trees of life. I am certain we would find that many Oaks of Righteousness sprang up to affect generations to come from that small town in New York State. What a godly heritage. What history changing currents these are!

This river reached flood tide and went on to heal America of her wounds in what became the Second Great Awakening. Finney was one example as a forerunner to the attainment of the full manifest glory of God for our time and for our generation. This is our destiny—our heritage. As in previous times, it is the real purpose for our existence.

It is the conviction of many in our time that the river of God is rising, that we have entered a time when it will rain so torrentially from the heavens, and a subterranean river of revelation and understanding will rise with such force that, **"... the glory of the Lord shall cover the earth as the waters cover the sea." Habakkuk 2:14**

We are in for a Third Great Awakening. Can it really be that God does not hear the cries of the desperate and the needy in our time? God forbid, or as our friend, Bishop William Frey says, "I am a prisoner of hope." May God's Healing River flood our generation and wash us onto the shores of His glory.

> **Then the angel showed me the river of the water of life, bright as crystal, flowing from the throne of God and of the Lamb through the middle of the street of the city. On either side of the river, is the tree of life with its twelve kinds of fruit, producing its fruit each month; and the leaves of the tree are for the healing of the nations.**
>
> **Rev. 22:1-2**

End Notes

1. Witnesses to the Holy Spirit: An Anthology, Judson Press (Valley Forge, PA. 1978) p. 96

2. Augustine, City of God, XXII, 8, Tr. By G. Walsh and D. Honan. (New York: Fathers of the Church, 1954) p. 310.

3. Witnesses to the Holy Spirit, p. 122.

4. Witnesses to the Holy Spirit, pp. 123-124.

5. The History of St. Cuthbert by Charles, Archbishop of Glasgow, (London: Burns and Oates, Limited. New York: Catholic Publication Society Co., 1887, pp. 28-29)

Order Form

God's Healing River: # of books @ $13.95 each = $_____

Under Healing Wings: # of books @ $15.95 each = $_____

The Genesis Seed: # of books @ $17.95 each = $_____

    Less 20% discount with 10 or more = $_____

    Subtotal = $_____

    Tax = 8.25% (Texas residents only) = $_____

Shipping and handling ($4.05 for first book,
  add $0.85 for each additional copy) $_____

(For bulk purchases email for shipping discount) $_____

                TOTAL ORDER $_____

Send check to:
The Rev. Dr. Jack Sheffield
Deep River Ministries
P.O. Box 12615
San Antonio, TX 78212

E-mail: *deepriver_@syahoo.com*
Website: *www.deepriverministries.com*

Ship to:

_____
(Name)

_____
(Street address)

_____
(City, State, Zip)

_____